COACHING DEFENSIVE LINE

FRITZ SHURMUR

Harding Press
Haworth, New Jersey 07641

Copyright © 1997 *by*

Fritz Shurmur

All rights reserved. This book may not be reproduced in any form or by any means without permission in writing from the publisher, except that permission is hereby given for reproduction of the scouting forms in Chapter 10.

Library of Congress Cataloging-in-Publication Data

Shurmur, Fritz.
  Coaching the defensive line / Fritz Shurmur.
     p.   cm.
  ISBN 0-9624779-8-2
    1. Line play (Football)   2. Football—Defense.   3. Football—
—Coaching. I. Title.
GV951.2.S58   1997
796.332'23—dc21   96-48256
                                                                                       CIP

ISBN: 0-9624779-8-2

Printed in the United States of America
HARDING PRESS
P. O. Box 141
Haworth, NJ 07641
Books by and for the coaching profession

Dedication

To the memory of my brother, Dr. Joe Shurmur. His life was one of caring and giving. And, although he enjoyed all the good things of life, especially family and friends, he gave so much more than he took. It is hard to describe how much we miss him. We are comforted somewhat in knowing the multitude of lives he affected so positively.

To Peggy Jane, whose patience, understanding and support through all the good and especially the not-so-good times make her an incredibly special coach's wife and mother. To our kids—Sally Ann the writer, Scott the doctor, and Susie the teacher—who have been and always will be great sources of pride to us.

To my mother and father, Len and Katie Shurmur, who worked and sacrificed all their lives to give me opportunities they never had.

To the many coaches and players I have been privileged to work with over the years. They are the reason going to work every day has been so enjoyable.

Contents

About the Author ix
Foreword xiii
Introduction xiv

1 PHYSICAL AND MENTAL REQUISITES 1

2 STANCE 3

Feet • 3
Hands and Arms • 5
Weight Distribution • 8

3 TEACHING THE HANDS 11

Striking the Blow • 11
Phases for Teaching the Hands • 16

4 TEACHING THE FOREARM 25

Forearm Technique • 25
Gap Technique • 27
Slant Technique • 29

5 TEACHING SHADES OR ALIGNMENTS AND KEYS   31

Defensive Alignment Designations • 31
Nose Tackle—Odd Spacing • 32
Defensive Tackles—Even Spacing • 34
Defensive Ends • 39
Summary • 44

6 BASIC FRONTS: APPLYING DEFENSIVE LINE ALIGNMENTS TO DEFENSIVE SCHEMES   45

The 4-3 Versus Strongside Run Formations • 45
The 4-3 Versus Weakside Run Formations • 47
The 4-3 Versus Balanced Formations • 50
4-3 Defense Versus Two Tight Ends • 52
4-3 Stack Defense • 52
4-3 Under Defense • 54
4-3 Over Defense • 56
3-4 Defense • 59
46 Defense • 61
Summary • 63

7 RUSHING THE PASSER   65

Objectives of the Rusher • 65
Fundamentals of the Pass Rush • 67
Straight Lines • 68
Feet • 69
Hands • 69
Head-Up Corner, or Edge, of the Blocker • 70
Phases of the Pass Rush • 72
Additional Points for the Pass Rusher • 76
Basic Pass-Rush Techniques • 78

8 LINE-CHARGE VARIATIONS: GAMES AND STUNTS 89

Execution of the Slant, or Gap, Technique • 90
Stunts—Linemen and Inside Linebackers • 93
Stunts—Linemen and Outside Linebackers • 96
Games Between Defensive Linemen • 97
Three-Man Games • 106
Summary • 107

9 DEFENSIVE LINE DRILLS 109

Warm-Up • 109
Movement Drills • 110
Sled Drills • 119
Pass-Rush Sled Drills • 122
Run—One-on-One Drills • 125
One-on-One Pass Rush—Head-Up Rushes • 126
One-one-One—Outside Pass Rushes • 129
Two-on-Two—Two-Man Games • 130
Three-Man Games • 130

10 DEFENSIVE LINE CHECKLIST AND OPPONENT EVALUATION FORM 133

(Reproducible checklists that can be copied and enlarged for use.)
Defensive Line Checklist • 133
Defensive Line Opponent Evaluation Form • 135

Acknowledgments

My sincere thanks to Gilbert Brown, Bob Kuberski and Gabe Wilkins, three exceptional football players, for their efforts and patience in the photography of the techniques and drills used in this book.

Thanks also to Carol Daniels for her assistance in the typing of this manuscript. I marveled at her ability to unscramble my hurried and, at times, illegible writing.

To Bob Eckberg and Al Treml for their assistance with the photographs used in the book. They are really good at what they do.

To Brian Nehring for his efforts to get all the sleds and other equipment in "Just the right place." He is a really dedicated professional.

To John Green and the Rogers Athletic Company for providing the sleds and agile pads. They are superb teaching devices.

To Eddie White and Logo Athletics for all their help in providing gear for the participants. They produce top-notch gear.

To the Green Bay Packers and Harmann Studios for providing the photo for the front cover of this book.

And last, but certainly not least, my thanks to my wife, Peggy Jane, for her help. She has a special way to "find a better word" or come up with a "better way of saying it" or, after reading it, saying "That's pretty good."

About the Author

An innovator, author and technician, as well as pro football's elder statesman in terms of service as a defensive coordinator, resourceful Fritz Shurmur has gained wide recognition over a distinguished career for his creative defensive schemes and masterful game plans.

Now in his 17th year as a coordinator, Shurmur, during the 1995 season, once again demonstrated his ability to develop both long- and short-term "solutions" to problems. In the former, he saw his defense force 56 three-and-out series over the 1995 season, the most in the National Football League.

In the latter, he devised an aggressive game plan that short-circuited San Francisco's vaunted passing game in the divisional playoffs, one that saw Packer defenders trigger and convert a receiver's fumble into a touchdown on the game's opening series and then constantly harry quarterback Steve Young, sacking him three times and forcing two interceptions en route to a highly convincing 27–17 victory in the 49ers' own 3Com Park.

The genial Michigan native, in his third season in Green Bay and his 22nd in the NFL overall, lost no time in putting his personal stamp upon the defensive platoon when named coordinator by Head Coach Mike Holmgren on January 31, 1994. Despite the injury-enforced retirements of linebacker Johnny Holland and right cornerback Roland Mitchell—and voluntarily confining himself to the scheme of predecessor Ray Rhodes in the interests of a smooth and effective transition—Shurmur presided over a defense that finished the 1994 season fifth in the National Football Conference and a highly respectable sixth in the league as a whole. His defenders then climaxed those efforts in the postseason by setting an all-time playoff record in their wild-card game against Detroit, holding the redoubtable Barry Sanders and the Lions to negative rushing yardage en route to a 16–12 victory in Green Bay's Lambeau Field. In that performance, the Packers held the Lions to minus 4 yards in 15 attempts, breaking a 31-year-old playoff record while restricting league rushing champion Sanders to a career-low minus 1 yard in 13 attempts.

Shurmur earlier demonstrated a classic example of his flair for innovation in 1989 when, as defensive coordinator for the Los Angeles Rams, he was confronted with the challenge of revamping an injury-depleted defensive unit. Utilizing linebackers as down linemen and compensating for the absence of two regular inside linebackers until the season's tenth game, he developed a 2-5 "Eagle" defense that allowed only three running backs to gain 100 yards, finished fifth in the NFC with 42 quarterback sacks and led the Rams to two postseason victories.

On the Phoenix staff for three years prior to joining the Packers, he produced comparable results in becoming the Cardinals' defensive coordinator in 1991. Developing a unit featuring seven new starters, he turned out a defense that held opponents to 52 fewer points than the previous season and limited the opposition to two touchdowns or less on nine occasions, scored three touchdowns on turnovers and shared the league low for touchdown passes allowed, with 12.

Shurmur's "11 men to the football" concept also triggered 37 fumbles, the third-highest single-season total in franchise history, while the Cardinals' 21 fumble recoveries ranked second in the NFC and third in the league.

A year later, his schematic originality paid dividends for Phoenix with a "Big Nickel" alignment that featured four down linemen, two linebackers and five defensive backs. It fueled a defensive surge that limited foes to 67.5 yards rushing per game over the final six weeks of the season and enabled the Big Red to finish with the fifth-rated defense in the conference. The unit also held opponents to 101 first downs, the best effort in club history over a 16-game schedule.

The following season, 1993, Shurmur's 4-2-5 Cardinal defense again proved highly effective, closing out the season seventh in the NFL in points allowed, with 269—an average of

16.9 per game—the team's lowest total since the 16-game schedule was implemented in 1978.

Shurmur had joined the Cardinals following nine seasons with the Los Angeles Rams' successful defense, eight of them as its coordinator. He signed on as the Rams' defensive line coach for the strike-shortened 1982 season and became their defensive coordinator the following year, in which the Rams improved from 27th to 15th in total defense. In 1985 and 1986, his efforts continued to bear fruit as the Rams led the NFL with 56 quarterback sacks in 1985 and finished fifth in total defense both seasons. Overall, the Rams qualified for postseason play six times during Shurmur's nine-year tenure.

The 64-year-old Wyandotte, Michigan, native made his NFL coaching debut with the Detroit Lions in 1975 as defensive line coach. He later was named the Lions' defensive coordinator in 1977. Four seasons in New England, the last two as defensive coordinator, followed. During this span, his 1979 Patriot defense led the NFL with 57 sacks.

Shurmur launched his coaching career in 1954 as a graduate student at his alma mater, Albion (Michigan) College, where he served as assistant football coach and swimming coach through 1961 before moving to the University of Wyoming as an assistant football coach. He was the Cowboys' defensive line coach from 1962–1970 prior to being named head coach in 1971. As Wyoming's defensive coach, Shurmur's teams led the nation in rushing defense twice and in total defense once. During his stay in Laramie, the Cowboys paced the Western Athletic Conference in defense in 1963 and from 1965–1969.

Blessed with writing skills to complement his football knowledge, Shurmur has authored three books—*Coaching Team Defense*, which covers all phases of defensive football and has elicited acclaim from his peers and fans alike; *The Eagle Five-Linebacker Defense*; and *Coaching Team Defense, Second Edition*.

Born July 15, 1932, Leonard "Fritz" Shurmur attended Roosevelt High School in his native Wyandotte. He later earned All-Michigan Athletic Association honors as a center at Albion College and was named the conference's most valuable player. Shurmur, who graduated with a master's degree in education administration in 1956, also was named to the all-conference baseball team.

Shurmur and his wife, Peggy Jane, have three children— Sally Ann Michalov, 39; Scott, 37; and Susie, 33. Sally Ann, an award-winning sports reporter for the *Casper Star-Tribune*, was named the 1990 Wyoming "Sportswriter of the Year."

Coaching Background: 1956–61 (Albion); 1962–74 (Wyoming, head coach, 1971–74); 1975–77 (Detroit Lions); 1978–81 (New England Patriots); 1982–90 (Los Angeles Rams); 1991–93 (Phoenix Cardinals); 1994–present (Green Bay Packers).

Foreword

I have watched and competed against Fritz Shurmur-coached teams for almost twenty years and have always admired and respected the way his defenses are played and put together.

Fritz is on the short list of top defensive minds in football. He has always broken down and simplified to his players complex schemes and, more importantly, made them playable. His books have done the same. *Coaching Team Defense* was and is a must for all coaches, players and even fans who want to understand *real football*.

Coaching the Defensive Line does for line play what his previous books have done in explaining defensive philosophy. All football starts up front with line play. This book teaches how to win those pit battles. From basic fronts, proper stance and drills, to the mental preparation needed, Fritz Shurmur covers all there is to know about defensive line play.

This is another must read for all coaches and fans of fundamental football. It's a terrific tool for coaches at any level. In addition, I highly recommend it to all football broadcasters…so that they too will know what they're talking about.

This book is the "Bible" of defensive line play.

Matt Millen
Television Football Analyst
Fox Sports

Introduction

I don't believe there is a more important group of players on a football team than the defensive linemen. Over the years it has become increasingly clear to me that the defensive teams that have the best chance of dominating their opponents are those with good defensive lines. If a defensive team can dominate and control their opponent's offensive line, they usually win. When this happens, there are no gaps in which to run the ball and limited time for the passer to throw the ball.

I also believe that average athletes, from the standpoint of size and athletic ability, can become great achievers with the acquisition of sound fundamentals and techniques. Good coaches who are good teachers can make good defensive linemen. Obviously, the best-equipped players athletically can achieve at the highest levels. However, players who possess average ability can also play at a high level.

The most important characteristic a defensive lineman must possess is physical toughness. Since defensive linemen will be involved in some type of contact on every play, it takes a player who is naturally aggressive to function well in this type of environment. He has to enjoy the contact aspect and the opportunity to attack the offensive blocker over him on every down.

1

Physical and Mental Requisites

Movement, or the ability to run, is a physical attribute essential to playing well on the line of scrimmage. Speed and quickness are the types of movement we are referring to here. The ability to run, accelerate off blocks and take off are all aspects of movement that are important.

Overall body strength is certainly very high on the list of physical qualities a defensive player must possess. The type of strength we are talking about here is what I like to call explosive strength. This is strength that the athlete can use while he is playing football. He can hit with power as he reacts to movement on the line of scrimmage or takes on a blocker as he pursues the ball carrier or defeats a blocker as he rushes the passer.

Associated with strength is leverage. Leverage is the ability to use the big muscles—the muscles of the lower body. Leverage is especially important to defensive linemen since it is the one factor that usually determines whether or not an offensive or defensive player wins the one-on-one battles that occur on the line of scrimmage. Elevation is the factor that usually determines the player who has the leverage advantage on a particular play. In a one-on-one confrontation, the player with the leverage advantage, and therefore the strength advantage, is the player whose shoulder level is lower than the other.

Strength in the hands and arms is another factor that is very important to defensive linemen. Players with strength in these areas will be adept at grabbing, turning, throwing and therefore escaping from blockers as they go to the ball carrier or passer.

Instinct, or the feel for where the blockers are coming from or where the ball is going, is also a quality I have observed in most players who succeed as defensive linemen. I do think that to a degree this is a natural, or inherent, characteristic, but I also believe it can be developed, or nurtured, or enhanced, with good coaching and experience.

The chapters that follow present what I feel are the important factors involved in playing at a high level on the defensive line of scrimmage. I also detail the techniques, methods of teaching and drills as well as the schemes I have used over the years. It is my belief you will receive a really good return on the investment in time you have spent reading this book.

2

Stance

Every play starts with the defensive lineman lining up in a stance. The stance is the starting point, and the type of stance a player uses determines how well he executes his responsibilities. Takeoff, elevation, leverage and the ability to use his hands, defeat the blocker and accelerate off blocks are all affected by the stance the player uses.

FEET

The feet should be pointed toward the path the player is planning to follow to execute his responsibilities. If he is an inside player whose base responsibilities take him on a straight-ahead path, the toes of both feet should be pointed in that direction in his stance. If, on the other hand, his responsibilities require him to point in or toward the ball, the toes of both feet should be pointed accordingly. This pointing of the feet is crucial to the proper alignment of linemen in their stances and varies all the way from a nose tackle whose feet would point straight ahead, to a wide defensive end whose feet might be pointing him in a forty-five degree angle to the line of scrimmage. (See Photos 2-1 and 2-2.)

Another important aspect of the feet, related to stance, is the relationship between the feet side-to-side and front-to-back. Usually the wider the feet are spread side-to-side, the closer they

PHOTO 2-1
Stance: Head-on view,
toes pointed straight ahead

PHOTO 2-2
Stance: Toes pointed at 45-degree angle with the line of scrimmage

are front-to-back. The feet should never be wider than shoulder width and never be closer than toe-to-heel. That is, the toe of the back foot should line up with the heel of the front foot. The foot that is back should always be to the side of the hand the player puts on the ground in a three-point stance. For example: For a right-handed player, that is, one who puts his right hand down, the right foot should be the back foot. One foot should always be back even if there is only a slight stagger as described above. The push-off or takeoff required to attack the offensive linemen requires this type of relationship. The bunched or tight stance described above is the type usually used by inside players like defensive tackles or nose tackles. These players have responsibilities that usually require side-to-side as well as straight-ahead responses. Players who use this type of stance usually align over an offensive lineman either head up or shading him slightly either inside or outside. Defensive linemen who use slant or angle charges on a regular basis use this type of stance as well.

Defensive linemen who line up in gaps or in space, like wide-aligned defensive ends, will usually use a more elongated stance. In this type of stance the feet are close together side-to-side but much farther apart front-to-back, and the emphasis is on up-the-field movement as opposed to lateral, or side-to-side. This type of stance is used more by pass rushers or players whose responsibilities require them to penetrate gaps rather than to take on and defeat offensive linemen. In all the types of stances discussed above, the player's weight should be distributed equally over the front portion, or balls, of each foot.

HANDS AND ARMS

Generally speaking, right-handed players will use a right-handed stance (right hand on the ground) and left-handed players a left-handed stance (left hand on the ground). However, it is possible for a right-handed player to learn and to effectively utilize a left-handed stance and vice-versa. For some players, using both a right-handed and left-handed stance is a relatively easy thing to do. For others it is very difficult and for some, impossible.

I think it is desirable for players who play on the left side of the defensive line to use a right-handed stance and for those who play on the right side to use a left-handed stance. The reason for this is that, as the player steps with his back foot, it brings him to a position where his inside leg is up, thereby putting him in a squared-up position with the line of scrimmage. This allows him to play with his inside leg up and his outside leg back, or away, from any blocker from his inside.

A nose tackle, or a player lined up over the center, can use a right- or left-handed stance with equal effectiveness.

It has been my experience that the execution of almost every technique used by linemen is enhanced by players in right-handed stances playing on the left side and vice-versa. I have also found that if a player tries to change his stance and is uncomfortable trying to play with it, the best plan is to let him go back to his old stance and modify it to make it more effective. For example, a player in a right-handed stance playing on the right side must learn to play with a normal step with the right foot and a short step or shuffle with the left foot. This allows the player to end up with the inside, or left, leg as the forward leg just as it would have been had he started in a left-handed stance. (See Photos 2-3, 2-4 and 2-5.)

PHOTO 2–3
Right-handed stance, side view

PHOTO 2–4
Right-handed stance, head-on view

PHOTO 2–5
Left-handed stance

I really do not think it makes any difference whether the player places his knuckles or the tips of his fingers on the ground. I think this is a simple matter of player comfort.

The off hand, or the one not on the ground, should hang loosely parallel with the hand on the ground. The tips of the fingers should be a few inches from the ground. The elbow or forearm should never rest on the player's leg. This position of the arm and hand places the hand in the most advantageous position for a player to use it most effectively in the execution of his techniques.

WEIGHT DISTRIBUTION

The amount of weight a player puts on his hand in his stance is determined by the type of charge he is going to use. If he is a penetrating, upfield type of player, he will have a great amount of weight forward, or on his hand. In this type of stance his legs will be relatively straight and his buttocks will be slightly higher

PHOTO 2–6
Bunched stance, weight evenly distributed

PHOTO 2–7
Elongated stance, most weight on hand

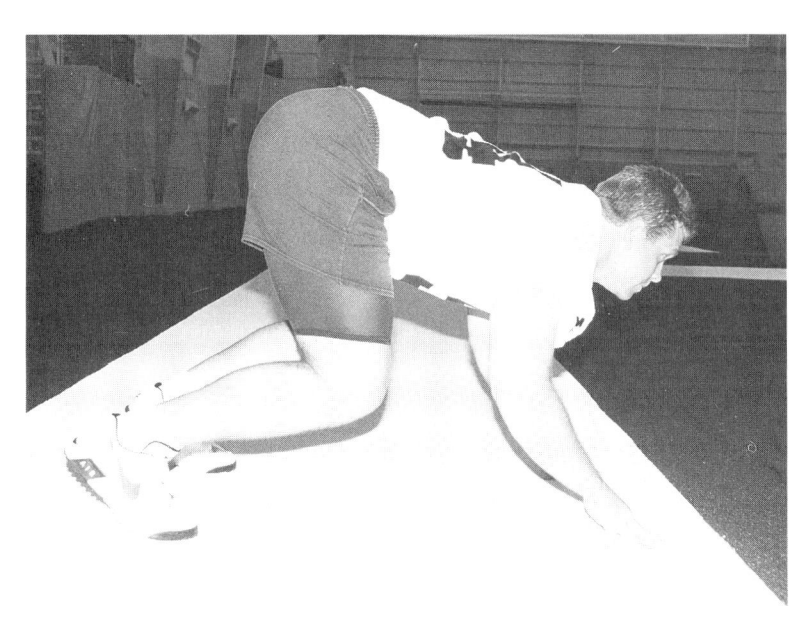

PHOTO 2–8
Four-point bunched stance, short yardage and goal line

than his shoulders. If he is a two-gap, or slanting, type of player, he is more inclined to have more weight back, or on his feet, with his knees bent more and his buttocks slightly lower than his shoulders. There are obviously varying degrees of both types of stances and to some degree player comfort plays a part in determining the exact stance used. (See Photos 2-6 and 2-7.)

The stances described above are all three-point, that is, the player has both feet and one hand on the ground. Some defenses, like short-yardage or goal-line defenses, require that the player use a four-point stance. In this type of stance both hands are on the ground, the buttocks are much higher than the shoulders and the elbows are bent. The player is attempting to assume a position as low as he can in this type of stance in order to drive under the offensive blocker and penetrate. (See Photo 2-8.)

3

Teaching the Hands

At any level of football the defensive linemen who are the most effective are really proficient in using their hands to defeat and shed blockers and to gain operating space in which to pursue the ball carrier or rush the passer. It is also a fact that, without a doubt, the person coaching defensive linemen must be really good at teaching this skill. After decades of personal experience coaching defensive linemen, at both the collegiate and professional levels, I have concluded that the ability to use his hands is the number-one technique a defensive lineman must acquire. I also believe that the ability to teach this technique is the number-one quality a defensive line coach must possess.

I am convinced that, within reason, any player can be taught to use his hands effectively as a defensive lineman. Even those players with marginal athletic skills can become adept at using their hands and, as a result, learn to be effective and achieve at a high level.

STRIKING THE BLOW

The blow is struck with the palms and heels of the hands. I don't really believe it makes a lot of difference whether the thumbs are pointed in toward each other or up. It has been my experience that most players are somewhere in between pointed straight in or straight up.

Aiming Point

The ideal place to strike a blow on the opponent is to place the hands on the upper outside edges of his front numbers. However, where the blow is actually struck on the opponent is really dependent upon the elevation of the blocker as he attempts to block the defender. One of the real advantages of the hands technique is that it is an adjustable technique. That is, the defensive lineman can be effective utilizing this technique to defeat the blocker and gain operating space regardless of the elevation or technique used by the offensive player as he attempts to block. The blow may be struck on the blocker anywhere from the upper tips of the front numbers, on a blocker attempting to block high, to the tips of the shoulders on one who is trying to scramble or cut block. (See Photos 3-1, 3-2 and 3-3.)

PHOTO 3-1
Rear view: Hands on tips of number on sled

PHOTO 3–2
Striking blow on the high blocker at tips of number

PHOTO 3–3
Adjusting hands to scramble the low blocker

Strength of the Blow

The strength of the blow comes from the quickness with which the blow is struck—straightening the arms, or locking out, and employing leverage, or the utilization of the big muscles of the body. All movement of the hands and arms should be forward—there should be no hitching or winding up. I believe it is much like a fighter throwing a quick jab or six-inch punch. With a quick punch the fighter has a good chance of landing his punch and being effective. If, however, he tries to reach back or wind up and land a haymaker, his opponent is more than likely going to land a punch on his chin while he is winding up. The same is true in using the hands—if the defensive lineman drives the hands at the opponent quickly with no hitching or winding up, he is more inclined to land his blow and not only stop the forward motion of the blocker but drive him back. If, however, he hitches or delays the forward movement of his hands, the opponent will likely have moved his body mass toward the defender and made contact on the defensive side of the line of scrimmage. When this happens, the defensive lineman is usually knocked off the line of scrimmage and, as a result, defeated by the offensive blocker.

Locking Out

As the player's hands make contact with the opponent, he must work to straighten his arms, or lock out, at the elbows. This locking-out process causes the large muscles of the back to be involved in the technique and therefore increases the strength or force of the blow. If the arms remain bent at the elbows, the strength of the blow is reduced significantly. With arms bent the biceps and triceps are the primary source of power.

This straightening, or locking-out, process also serves to provide the defensive player with operating space or separation from the blocker. The defender is therefore better able to use his hands to rush the passer or shed the blocker and pursue the ball carrier. (See Photo 3-4.)

PHOTO 3-4
Side view of hands technique, locking out on sled

Leverage

Simultaneous with the locking-out process should come the involvement of the big muscles below the waist. They become part of the blow being struck due to the defensive lineman bending at ankles, knees and hips. This flexion in these areas contributes to the force and power of the blow. In addition to bending in these areas, the other factor involved in leverage is elevation. Usually the player who plays lower will have better big-muscle involvement, or leverage. Defensive linemen will almost always win the battle of power, strength or leverage if their shoulder level is lower than that of their opponent.

PHASES FOR TEACHING THE HANDS

The most effective way to teach any technique is to utilize the part, or phase, method of teaching. I know of no other technique associated with football that lends itself more readily to this method than the hands.

The best way to begin teaching the hands technique to players is on a sled or shiver board. The best type of sled is one that utilizes wide, relatively flat pads with numbers similar to the numbers on the front of a player's jersey. A shiver board is usually a 2-×-12 board padded with some type of soft sponge or Styrofoam material and covered with canvas or vinyl. This board can be hung from a sled or mounted on a wall, fence or posts that are anchored in the ground. Any of these devices should have its center about three feet from the ground. This will allow players of varying heights to have a reasonable target to strike with the hands.

The Knees

Starting players on their knees is beneficial for several reasons, the most significant of which is that it completely isolates the hands and arms or the striking part of the technique. It also ensures that the player will operate on a lower plane than he would if he were in a stance. In addition, the player can devote his complete attention, or focus, on target without worrying about stepping as well as striking. The player should first assume a position on his knees in front of the sled or board with his back relatively straight, his arms hanging loosely in front of him, his head and eyes focused on the target, which is the outer upper tips of the numbers on the pad on the sled. (See Photo 3-5.)

Locking out

Next, he should get a fit, that is, place the palms and heels of his hands on the upper outside edges of the numbers. He should then straighten his arms, or lock out, which kicks in or involves the muscles of the back. At this point it should be

PHOTO 3-5
Knees on sled, ready to strike blow

PHOTO 3-6
Hands: Fit on the sled from the knees

demonstrated to the player that, if he does not lock the elbows, his primary strength will come only from his biceps. He should be able to feel the additional power generated by the involvement of the big muscles of the back. (See Photo 3-6.)

Rolling the hips

After he has locked out a few times, the player should then be encouraged to get a fit with the hands, lock out and then roll the hips into the blow by bringing them forward. By the proper placement of the hands (or fit), the locking of the arms and the rolling of the hips, the player should develop a feel for the tremendous power he can generate in a blow when all the elements of the technique are applied. The phase method of teaching allows these isolated portions of the technique to be identified by the player. (See Photo 3-7.)

Maintaining constant head and eye level

As all of these phases are being taught, the player's head and shoulder level should be monitored. Once he has estab-

PHOTO 3–7
Knees: Lock out and roll hips in

lished a level with his eyes focused on the target straight ahead, he should maintain that level all the way through the execution of the technique. Again, a head and shoulder level lower than his opponent's always ensures a leverage advantage.

Striking the blow

The next phase is also executed from the knees. On the movement of the ball, the player strikes the sled with his hands and, as he does, works to lock out at the elbows and at the same time roll his hips into the blow. It must be emphasized that the strength of the blow comes from three important factors. One is the quickness with which the blow is struck, the second is the locking of the elbows and the third is the rolling of the hips. The player executing this technique should be encouraged to hold this power position with his hands on the sled to really get the feel of executing the technique. This prevents the player from slapping the sled rather than driving the hands to and through the sled, which is really what we are trying to develop. Again, it is important that all movement of the hands and arms be forward. There should be no winding up or hitching of the hands.

On the Sled from a Three-Point Stance

After the player has developed a feel for the hands technique from his knees, the next step is to go through the same progression on the sled from a three-point stance.

Again, it all starts from the knees. The player lines up in a three-point stance in front of the sled. He then places his hands on the tips of the numbers for a fit, locks out and rolls his hips. At this point he does not move his feet. (See Photo 3-8.)

After the player has the feel of the fit, lock out and rolling of the hips, the next phase involves the player, from a stance, striking a blow on the movement of a ball by the coach. Again, we are emphasizing that the defender strike the blow on the sled, as quickly as possible, with the hands and with no movement of the feet. All elements of the blow should be executed including the locking out at the elbows and the rolling of the hips into the blow. Again, the elevation of the shoulders and eyes should remain constant throughout the blow.

PHOTO 3-8
Hands: Fit on sled from stance (up position)

The final phase of teaching the hands technique on the sled involves the player, on movement by the coach, striking a blow from a stance, locking out, rolling the hips and then finishing with a short step so he ends up with his inside leg closer to the offensive side of the line of scrimmage in a slight toe-to-heel stagger. (See Photo 3-9.)

Emphasize striking first

In all these phases it is important to emphasize to the player the value of the defensive lineman attacking the offensive lineman with his hands. He has to be convinced that the hands alone can get to the offensive blocker faster than the hands and the feet working simultaneously can. If a player tries to step and to strike with the hands at the same time, he will not be as quick to get to the blocker. Going after the blocker with the hands allows the defender to attack the blocker on the offensive side of the line of scrimmage. This allows the defender to play the game on the offensive side of the line of scrimmage. Trying to

PHOTO 3-9
Striking blow with hands and finishing with inside leg (left leg) up

step and strike simultaneously ensures that the momentum of the offensive blocker will cause the defender to catch rather than attack the blocker and thus lose the battle on the line of scrimmage.

Versus a Live Blocker

After the hands technique has been taught on the sled or shiver board, the next step is to teach the phases of the technique versus a live blocker. It is best to use other defensive players as blockers in this drill. The offensive lineman is a passive player or a target in this phase of the teaching process. It is most effective if the defensive lineman begins the drill in a three-point stance, and the offensive blocker lines up with his hands on his knees in a two-point stance.

The initial phase of this drill involves the defensive lineman striking with the hands, on the tips of the numbers of the offensive lineman and driving him back. All the phases of locking out at the elbows and rolling the hips should be applied. This drill should progress from little or no resistance from the blocker to a considerable amount of pressure or resistance from the offensive player. It is important that the defensive lineman be encouraged to drive or walk the player back. During this process, it is essential that the defensive player maintain a leverage advantage by keeping his shoulder and face-mask level lower than that of his opponent throughout the execution of the technique. (See Photo 3-10.)

After the defensive lineman has executed the hands technique in this fashion, the next phase involves the offensive lineman coming off the ball from a stance. Again, the velocity with which the blocker comes off should be increased until it simulates an actual one-on-one block by an offensive lineman on a running play.

PHOTO 3–10
Fit with hands on offensive blocker's numbers

Finish with the shed

The next phase is the finish of the technique, which involves getting rid of the blocker, or the shed. After the defensive lineman has defeated the blocker and knocked him back, the next phase is the shed. With this phase, as soon as the ball carrier commits to a side, the defensive lineman sheds, or throws, the offensive lineman in the opposite direction from which the ball carrier commits, accelerates up the field or toward the ball carrier and proceeds in a path to make the tackle. It is important for the defensive lineman to know that he continues to knock the offensive player back until the ball carrier commits to a side, either to the right or left of the blocker. This knocking-back process causes the ball carrier to make a decision on a cut quicker than he wants to, which in turn decreases or reduces the cutback angles. It is important that the defensive lineman, as he throws, or sheds, the offensive player, use this momentum to work upfield and thus decrease the options or cutback angles the ball carrier has at his disposal.

These drills may eventually evolve into tackling drills off of the two-gap technique.

4

Teaching the Forearm

The hands technique must be the primary method of striking a blow that is taught to defensive linemen. However, there are times when the use of the forearm, as a technique, is absolutely essential.

FOREARM TECHNIQUE

Generally speaking, the forearm is used in situations when the defensive lineman is lined up in an inside technique, short-yardage or goal-line, or the defensive lineman is in a position where he has to take on and defeat a blocker who has momentum or a run at the defensive lineman. Wham blocks, lead blocks or trap blocks are examples of the types of blocks where the forearm technique may be the most effective one to use.

In the execution of the forearm technique, utilization of body position, leverage and the feet is the same as it is for the hands technique.

The forearm blow is delivered with the back of the hand and the top of the forearm. As in the hands technique, all movement of the hand and arm is forward. There is no winding up or hitching. The blow is struck under the shoulder pads of the offensive blocker. Again, the defensive player is always in an advantageous position if his shoulder level is lower than that of the offensive blocker. The blow is a rip up through the blocker. The defender should attempt to drive his arm through the blocker, following through with an upward motion of the forearm.

The off arm, or hand other than the one delivering the forearm blow, should be used to drive through the shoulder pad of the blocker to turn him or to grab the blocker to turn him to allow the defender to shed the blocker and go to the ball. Generally speaking, most blockers will be attacking defenders from the inside; therefore, most of the time defensive linemen will be using their inside arm, or the arm closest to the ball, to deliver the forearm blow. However, on occasion blockers will attack defensive linemen from the outside in. When this occurs, the outside arm is used to deliver the forearm blow. After the defensive player has defeated the blocker with the forearm, he must get his hands involved to shed the blocker.

PHOTO 4–1
Striking forearm blow on sled

As the blow is delivered, the defensive lineman must strive to maintain a squared-up relationship with the line of scrimmage—that is, his hips and shoulders should be parallel with the yard lines on the field. In order to maintain this relationship, the defensive lineman should always work to step with the leg to the side of the forearm he is striking with. In other words, if he is striking with the right forearm, he should be stepping with the right leg. This allows the defender to close the hole with the blocker, shed the block and make the tackle. I do not believe in the off-arm or cross-arm technique in which the defender uses his outside arm, turns his body and takes on a blocker attacking him from the inside. This trade one-for-one theory of defensive football, in my opinion, is not in any way sound. It violates every principle of defensive football I believe in. I have always been convinced that defensive players should be taught technique whereby they defeat blockers and, as a result, are in a position to get off the block and tackle the ball carrier. (See Photo 4-1.)

GAP TECHNIQUE

With the hands technique and the forearm technique the defensive lineman is attacking and working to defeat an offensive player. With the gap technique the defender is attempting to avoid contact on the line of scrimmage and penetrate in the gap between offensive linemen.

Usually with this technique, the defensive lineman assumes an elongated pass-rush type of stance in order to gain as much ground as possible upfield at the snap of the football. (See Photo 4-2.)

There are usually two types of techniques used in these situations. One is the short-yardage or aggressive technique used in short-yardage and goal-line situations. When a defensive lineman uses this technique, he usually uses a four-point stance, has his hips higher than his head and penetrates the gap at the snap of the ball. In these situations he leads through the gap with his shoulders, working to drive through the gap and work up through the blockers as he penetrates.

The other type of gap technique is the swim, or slap-and-go technique. When a defensive lineman engages in this type of

PHOTO 4-2
Gap-charge goal-line defense, interior linemen

penetration, at the snap of the ball he reaches for the shoulder pad of the offensive lineman, grabs his shoulder pad and pulls his body through the gap. He may do it with his inside or outside hand. The key here is that he keep his shoulder level lower than that of the offensive blocker as he pulls his body through the gap.

The defensive lineman then has two options for the use of the off arm. One is the rip-arm technique and the other is the swim technique.

The rip-arm technique involves the defender ripping the off arm through the gap while striving to maintain a shoulder level lower than that of the offensive blocker. Again, if the defensive lineman is grabbing with the right arm, the left arm is the off arm. The other technique that involves the off arm is the swim technique. With this technique the defender swims, or brings the off arm over the top of the offensive player as he penetrates the gap. This technique is much like the action utilized by a swimmer in doing the overhand crawl stroke. The problem with the swim, especially with young players, is that they raise up or compromise their leverage position when they use this technique. That is why I favor using the rip technique, especially with young players, since this technique puts the pressure on the defensive lineman to stay down all through the technique and not raise up and thereby compromise his leverage position.

SLANT TECHNIQUE

In slant defenses, or defenses where the defensive linemen line up in a position and move to another predetermined position at the snap of the ball, there are some very important technique factors involved.

The don'ts of this technique are probably as important as the do's. First, don't compromise the squared-up relationship (that is, hips and shoulders parallel with the line of scrimmage). Second, don't ever cross the feet over while executing the technique. And, third, but just as important, do not raise up or compromise the shoulder level while executing the technique.

Movement of a defensive lineman right or left or to the strongside or weakside of the formation is usually best accomplished by the defensive lineman lining up in a head-up position over an offensive lineman. However, for the purpose of disguise and the element of surprise, occasionally it is possible to execute the slant technique from an inside or outside shade alignment.

With the slant technique, at the snap of the ball the defensive lineman takes a flat parallel step with the foot in the direction he is going. The foot he is stepping with should be pointed toward the offensive line of scrimmage. As he steps, his shoulder level should stay the same as it was when he lined up in his stance. As he steps, the slanting defensive lineman should penetrate the gap and read and react to all blocks that are attacking him in the direction he is slanting. For example: A defensive end in a 3-4 defense, who is slanting inside, will react by squeezing any play designed to attack his side of the formation. If, however, he feels pressure from a down block by the offensive tackle, he must work back toward the outside where the play is designed to go. If the blockers are attacking him from the direction in which he is slanting, he should take on all blockers with the forearm or hands in the direction in which he is slanting. For example: Slant to the left, take on blockers from the inside with the left forearm; slant to the right, take on blockers with the right forearm. If the blockers attack the slanting lineman away from the direction in which he is slanting, he should use the forearm to the side from which the blockers are attacking him.

The second step in the slant technique should be a parallel step with the off foot, or the foot away from the direction in which the lineman is slanting. Again, this foot should be pointed upfield, or toward the line of scrimmage, as he penetrates the gap he is slanting to.

5

Teaching Shades or Alignments and Keys

DEFENSIVE ALIGNMENT DESIGNATIONS

Front

```
9 8 7 6 5 4 3 2 1 0 0 0 1 2 3 4 5 6 7 8 9
```

Center
0—Head On
O Strong—TE Side Eye
O Weak—Away from TE Eye

Guards
1—Inside Shade
2—Head On
3—Outside Shade

Tight End
7—Inside Shade
8—Head On
9—Outside Shade

Tackle
4—Inside Shade
5—Head On
6—Outside Shade

Gap Description

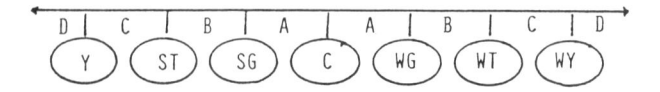

```
 D | C | B | A | A | B | C | D
   (Y)(ST)(SG)(C)(WG)(WT)(WY)
```

With each defense, the front seven personnel will be responsible for specific offensive gap responsibilities. Gaps are coded as follows:

STRONGSIDE A—From Center's nose to nose of Strongside Guard
STRONGSIDE B—From Strongside Guard's nose to nose of Strongside Tackle
STRONGSIDE C—From Strongside Tackle's nose to nose of TE (Y)
STRONGSIDE D—From Nose of TE (Y) out
WEAKSIDE A—From Center's nose to nose of Weakside Guard
WEAKSIDE B—From nose of Weakside Guard to nose of Weakside Tackle
WEAKSIDE C—From nose of Weakside Tackle to nose of WY
WEAKSIDE D—From nose of WY out

The type of defensive scheme utilized by a team is usually determined by the type of personnel it has. At the very foundation of this determination is the makeup of the defensive line. Generally speaking, the bigger, more physical type of defensive line dictates a two-gap, knock-'em-back scheme, while the smaller, quicker type of defensive line dictates a gap, penetrating mode with the defensive linemen.

NOSE TACKLE—ODD SPACING

O Technique—The Two-Gap Nose Tackle

The nose tackle aligned head up on the center is usually a two-gap player; that is, he is responsible for the A gap to the side the running play is designed to attack. His responsibilities are usually described as to knock the center back and defend the frontside or playside A gap. With an aggressive two-gap technique a nose tackle must understand that his primary responsibility is to knock the center back. This will allow him to play aggressively and play on the offensive side of the line of scrimmage. If he is reach-blocked by the center, the linebacker playing behind him will merely adjust his gap responsibility on runs away from him. With an O technique it is permissible for the nose tackle to get reach-blocked by the center, but he cannot be two-hatted. That is, he cannot be reach-blocked by the center and the guard.

The primary key of the O technique nose is the center's block, but he must also be aware of the action of the guard on either side of the center or any tight end or back who is in position to wham block him. This alignment and technique is the one usually employed by teams that use a 3-4, two-gap scheme. (See Photo 5-1.)

PHOTO 5–1
Head-up alignment

O Strong or Weak Technique—The Offset Nose

With the O strong or weak technique the nose tackle lines up on the shoulder of the center to the strongside or weakside of the offensive formation. This alignment is usually dictated by the defensive scheme. The nose tackle lines up with his feet, hips and shoulders parallel with the line of scrimmage. I do not believe in the cocked-nose type of offset alignment nor do I believe in teaching any type of technique that violates the basic principles of defensive linemen lining up and playing the game with a parallel relationship with the line of scrimmage.

In the execution of this technique the nose tackle attacks the near shoulder of the center with the hands technique. His gap responsibility requires that he defend the A gap he is lined up in on the offensive side of the line of scrimmage. He cannot be reach-blocked by the center on plays to his side of the center or reach-blocked by the guard on plays away. If both the center and guard block him, the nose tackle must work for penetration in the A gap and cannot be pushed to a position where he can be reach-blocked by either player.

The primary run keys of the offset nose tackle are the center and the guard to the side he lines up on.

This offset nose alignment technique is the one utilized by many teams that use the over or under, four-man-line types of defense. (See Photos 5-2 and 5-3.)

DEFENSIVE TACKLES—EVEN SPACING

2 Technique—The Two-Gap Tackle

The 2 technique involves the defensive tackles lining up head up on the offensive guards. The base responsibility of a player lined up in this position is to knock the guard back and defend the playside gap. That is, if the running play is designed to attack his side of the center, the tackle is responsible for the B gap. If the run is designed to attack the opposite side of the center, he is responsible for the A gap, or the area between him and the center. As is always the case, it is the job of the lineman

PHOTO 5-2
Offset nose or outside shade alignment—right-handed stance

PHOTO 5-3
Offset nose or outside shade alignment—left-handed stance

to knock an offensive lineman back and defend the playside gap—if there is a conflict, the most important job is to knock the offensive lineman back. If the guard should reach block with a flat parallel step thereby preventing the tackle from playing his frontside gap responsibility, the tackle continues to work upfield and let the linebacker work to the B gap. In other words, the action by the blocker causes the tackle and the middle linebacker to switch gap responsibilities as the play develops.

The primary key of the tackle lined up in a 2 technique is the guard he is lined up over. However, it is critically important that he see and react to the action of the center.

If the guard fires straight out at the tackle, he should use his hands technique, knock the guard back, read the play, shed the blocker and go to the ball. If the guard fires off the ball and tries to reach or cut off the tackle, he should knock the guard back and work to the playside gap. If the guard pass blocks, the tackle should rush the passer, as an inside rusher, on his side of the center.

With all running plays where the guard does not block the defensive tackle, the center becomes a very important key. His action tells the defensive tackle what type of running play he must be ready to defend. For example: If the center blocks the opposite tackle, his first threat is a trap from the inside. If a trap shows, he must close the trap with his inside leg and inside arm. His hips and shoulders should be parallel with the line of scrimmage. He should never take on this type of block by turning and using his outside, or off, arm. Again, I do not believe in any techniques that cause the defensive lineman to compromise his body's squared-up relationship with the line of scrimmage.

Also, a block back by the center could mean a wham play by a back or tight end. This type of block will occur from the outside of the tackle. The aligning of a potential whammer, a tight end or back either lined up or motioning to an outside wham position, is an alert that the tackle should be made aware of by the offensive formation. If a tight end or back whams with a block back by the center, the tackle should take on and defeat the blocker with his outside leg up, using either his outside forearm technique or hands to defeat the blocker.

If the center blocks back or blocks the opposite tackle on outside plays, the offensive tackle will usually block down on the defensive tackle. When this happens, the defensive tackle should break the line of scrimmage, flatten his route and try to get in front of the ball carrier running wide. The other option is to play through the block by the tackle squeezing the play from the inside. The defensive tackle should never give ground on this type of block. He must always play it by pressuring the offensive side of the line of scrimmage. On wide plays with the center blocking away, the block back by the center is the first key the tackle gets, the second is the block down by the offensive tackle and the third is the actual ball handling or action of the play. He must feel and see all three of these specific actions.

If the center blocks to the side of the defensive tackle, it will be a reach block, and the play will be designed to come his way or it will be a block back on a running play designed to go to the opposite side of the formation. If it is an inside play like a trap play, he should squeeze the center's block closing the hole with the center's body. If it is a wide play away from him, the tackle should either squeeze the center's block or, if his takeoff allows him to beat the center's block, he should flatten his route and work to get in front of the ball carrier.

3 Technique—Outside Shade on the Guard

This is commonly called an outside-eye or outside-shoulder technique. The inside eye of the defensive tackle is usually the part of the defensive player's anatomy that is used to align on the offensive player. In a wide 3 alignment the defensive tackle aligns in his stance with his inside eye opposite the tip of the outside shoulder of the offensive guard. In a tight 3 alignment the defensive tackle aligns with his inside eye lined up opposite the outside eye of the offensive guard.

The gap responsibility for a 3 technique player is the same on runs to his side of the formation as it is in a 2, or head-up, technique. That is, he is responsible for the B gap. On plays designed to be run away from him or to the opposite side of the formation, he is responsible for the B gap to his side of the formation. This is where his gap responsibility differs from that of a 2 technique. On running plays designed to go away from him, he has the additional responsibility of squeezing the A gap to his side of the formation with a cutoff block by the guard or block back by the center.

The defensive tackle lined up in a 3 technique should see the center as he does in a 2 technique and react to the actions of the center in a similar manner. However, on plays like trap plays the offensive guard will usually try to release off inside to block the middle linebacker.

The guard should be prevented from doing this if the defensive tackle leads with his hands and flattens the release of the guard as he tries to release to the inside. If the defensive tackle is lined up in a 2 alignment, the offensive guard will usually give the defensive tackle some type of pass-set or reach-block influence on inside trap plays.

The aiming points for the use of the hands technique are exactly the same as they are in a 2 technique—that is, the outside tips of the numbers on the front of the offensive guard.

1 Alignment—Inside Shade on the Guard

If an inside alignment is utilized by the defensive tackle, his outside eye is used for lining-up purposes. If a tight alignment is desired, the defensive tackle lines up with his outside eye opposite the inside eye of the offensive guard. The wide alignment has the outside eye of the tackle aligned opposite the inside shoulder of the offensive guard.

There are two basic rules that must be followed anytime an inside technique is used. One is that the lineman lined up on any type of inside shade must key and react to the block of the first offensive lineman lined up to his inside. For the defensive tackle, the key is the offensive center. If the center blocks back or away from the defensive tackle, he should close the trap or, if there is no trap, react to the block from his outside.

If the center tries to reach block him, the defensive tackle should work up the field, defend the A gap and pursue the ball.

The second rule he must follow is that he must feel and react to any block from the outside. The most frequent block he will get will be a down block by the offensive guard. On this type of play the running play is usually designed to go outside to his side of the formation. With this type of block the defensive tackle will either beat the down block with his takeoff, flatten his route and pursue the play or squeeze the tackle's block from the inside-out. He should never spin out or give ground to play across this type of block because such reactions by the tackle make it very difficult for the linebacker playing behind him to maintain an up-and-in or downhill angle as he attacks the running play.

DEFENSIVE ENDS

5 Alignment—The Two-Gap End

The defensive end aligned head up on the offensive tackle is utilizing a 5 technique or two gap. This means his responsibility is to knock the offensive tackle back and defend the playside gap. That is, if the running play is designed to attack his side of the formation, he is responsible for the C gap. If, on the other hand, the play is designed to go to the opposite side of the formation, he is responsible for the B gap. The aiming point, or target, for hand placement by the defensive end is the outside upper tips of the front numbers of the offensive tackle.

The defensive end's first responsibility is to knock the tackle back on any drive block. If there is a conflict in his base responsibilities because the tackle steps flat to either reach block or cut him off, the defensive end must work up the field and flatten his route to the ball carrier.

If the offensive tackle doesn't block the defensive end and pulls outside or pass influences him, the end should first check inside for a blocker from the inside. If the near guard blocks him, the defensive end should squeeze the guard's block. If a puller or wham blocker attempts to block the defensive end, the end should close and defeat the blocker on the offensive side of the line of scrimmage.

If the tackle pulls outside and there is no block from the inside, the defensive end will probably be blocked from the outside by the tight end. He should squeeze the block of the tight end by working through him upfield, or toward the offensive line of scrimmage. If the defensive end's takeoff causes the tight end to miss him, he should flatten his route as soon as he breaks the line of scrimmage and pursue the ball carrier.

If pass shows and the defensive end is lined up in a 5 alignment, immediately upon pass recognition he should work to the inside or outside corner of the blocker as he assumes a pass-rush mode. If, by the design of the defense, he is an outside pass rusher (that is, no other defender is assigned to rush the passer outside him) he should rush over the outside of the offensive tackle. However, in defensive schemes when there is a pass rusher outside him, he should use an inside pass-rush technique on the offensive tackle.

6 Alignment—Outside Shade on the Tackle

The aiming points for the hands with a 6 alignment are the same as with a 5 alignment. There are two primary differences in the responsibilities of a defensive end lined up in a 5 or 6. The first difference is that with a 5 alignment the defensive end may or may not be able to defend the C gap, depending on the type of block the offensive tackle uses on the defensive end. Whereas, with a 6 alignment the defensive end must guarantee that he will be a C gap player on runs his way. The other difference is that, on plays away, the defensive end squeezes the body of the offensive tackle into the B gap with a 6 alignment. Whereas, with a 5 alignment the defensive end should have his body in the B gap on plays away.

Almost all other situations, circumstances and reactions in a 6 alignment are the same as they are with a 5 alignment. The one big difference is with a 6 alignment on running plays that are designed to attack the B and A gaps to his side of the formation—with plays like traps and whams the offensive tackle will try to release inside, rather than pull or influence block.

4 Alignment—Inside Shade on the Offensive Tackle

The 4 alignment involves the defensive end lining up with his inside eye lined up opposite the inside shoulder of the offensive tackle. The defensive end should key and react to the action of the offensive guard. On any down block or pull away by the tackle, the end should close and squeeze at the next level. The next level is about a half yard to a full yard deep on the offensive side of the line of scrimmage. If the guard attempts to block him out, he should squeeze the block and remain in the B gap. On any block down by the tackle, the defensive end should either squeeze, working through the block, or beat the block with takeoff and flatten his route to the ball carrier.

I really do not favor the utilization of a 4 alignment in a defensive scheme. Anytime a player lines up in an inside shade, I feel his aggressiveness is hampered due to the fact that while keying and reacting to what he is seeing inside, the offensive tackle has the advantage of a good angle to block down on him on wide plays.

Wide 6 Alignment

Wide alignment is used by the defensive end on the open side of the formation in an under or 4-3 defense. The wide 6 alignment requires the defensive end to line up one and one-half yards outside the offensive tackle. He should be pointed in with the near hip of the near back as his aiming point. His keys are the triangle that consists of the near back, the offensive tackle and the pulling lane. The pulling lane is that area immediately behind the offensive line. This lane is about two yards in depth and is the area offensive linemen appear in when they are pulling to block for plays designed to attack the perimeter of the defense. Depending on the design of the scheme, the defensive end will be responsible for force or contain on running plays to his side of the formation or he will have a force man outside of him. How he reacts or plays the various types of blocks is dependent upon whether or not, by defensive design, he is the force man. If he is not responsible for force, he should two gap or play through the middle of the blocker, keeping his inside arm free. If he is responsible for the force, he should take on all blockers and defeat them on their side of the line of scrimmage, maintaining a force or outside position on the ball carrier. (See Photo 5-4.)

PHOTO 5–4
Wide 6 alignment, open side of defense

If the offensive tackle tries to block him out, the defensive end must squeeze the block and maintain his outside position.

If the near back or a blocker in the pulling lane attempts to block him, the defensive end should attack the blocker, defeat him and maintain his outside position if he is the force man. If he is not responsible for force, he should two gap or play through the middle of the blocker, keeping his inside arm free. If he is responsible for the force, he should take on all blockers by squeezing and maintaining his outside position on the blocker.

This particular alignment requires that the defensive end execute his responsibilities with speed. Great takeoff is absolutely essential. He wants to make things happen as deep as he can in the offensive backfield. For example: If a running back is trying to block the defensive end, ideally the contact between the blocker and the defender should take place one to two yards deep behind the line of scrimmage. If he is being blocked by a pulling lineman, the contact point should be about one yard deep. If the offensive tackle tries to block the defensive end out, he should squeeze or compress the block about a yard deep in the backfield. It is very important that the defensive end who lines up in a wide 6 alignment be coached to read, react and make things happen on the offensive side of the line of scrimmage. When a tackle tries to block him on a draw play by pushing him up the field, it is important that the defensive end drive his inside hand to the inside number on the front of the tackle's jersey. As he does this, he should work back to a squared-up position on the line of scrimmage, squeeze the tackle's block and hold his outside position.

8 Alignment—Head up, or Two Gap, on the Tight End

This alignment is usually used in some type of over defense. The defensive end lines up head up on the tight end. On the snap of the ball, the job of the defensive end is to knock the tight end back, shed the blocker and react to the play. The defensive end should defeat any one-on-one block by the tight end. If the tight end attempts to release inside, the defensive end should get his hands on him, flatten his release route and close inside while looking for blockers from the inside. If the tight end releases outside, the defensive end should attempt to flatten his outside release and close inside while looking for blockers from the inside. With either of these releases the defensive end should move to the next level or a position about a yard deep in the offensive backfield as he closes inside.

9 Alignment—Outside Shoulder of the Tight End

In a 9 alignment the defensive end lines up, slightly turned in, with his inside eye looking through the outside shoulder of the tight end into the core of the backfield. With this alignment the defensive end should squeeze or compress any block by the tight end as he attempts to block out. If the tight end tries to reach or hook block the defensive end, he should work up the field and maintain his outside position if he is the force man in the defensive design. If the defensive end is not the force man, he must either two gap the tight end up the field or, if the tight end overcommits to the outside, he may work upfield inside the block. If the tight end attempts to release inside, the defensive end should get his hands on him, flatten his course and proceed to close while looking for blockers from the inside.

7 Alignment—Inside Shoulder of the Tight End

The defensive end should line up with his outside eye looking through the inside shoulder of the tight end into the core of the backfield. As is the case with any inside alignment, the general rule is to key inside and feel any block from the outside. The defensive end should key the action of the offensive tackle. If the tackle blocks down or pulls away, the defensive end should close looking for blockers from the inside. If the tackle blocks him out, he should squeeze or compress the block maintaining his outside position in the C gap.

If the tight end blocks down on the defensive end, he should either squeeze, working through the block, or beat the block with takeoff and flatten his route to the ball carrier.

SUMMARY

When defensive linemen really understand how to line up in the alignments described above and learn how to execute their assignments from them, it makes possible the implementation of any type of defensive scheme. For example: If a defensive tackle learns how to line up in and execute the responsibilities from an O, O strong or O weak alignment, he is ready to be a nose tackle in a 3-4 defense or some type of over or under defense. If by the same token he is well versed in all that goes along with a 1, 2 or 3 alignment, he is ready to play a 4-3 or any type of even alignment.

If a defensive coaching staff starts with the basic objective of teaching the various alignments, it creates the opportunity to have a tremendous amount of flexibility in terms of the defensive fronts a team can employ over a season. If the defensive linemen really understand how to play the various techniques associated with these alignments, it enables a defensive team to make subtle alignment changes that allow them to take advantage of the strengths or weaknesses in offensive formations.

6

Basic Fronts: Applying Defensive Line Alignments to Defensive Schemes

THE 4-3 VERSUS STRONGSIDE RUN FORMATIONS

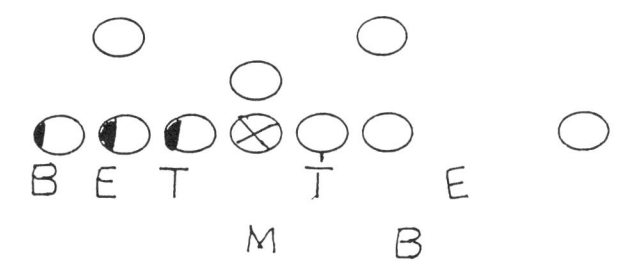

○   ○
 ○
◐◐◐⊗◐○   ○
B E T   T   E
    M   B

In a normal 4-3 defense the tackles determine how successful this front will be. In my opinion they are the key. They must be able to defeat the guards and control the middle versus the run. The alignments of the tackles must be adjusted to the run strength of the offensive formation. Versus offensive formations where the run strength is to the tight end, the tackles will move to the tight end. That is, the strongside tackle lines up in a tight 3 alignment. The weakside tackle, or the tackle away from the tight end, lines up in a 2 alignment.

Versus strongside running formations, the weakside defensive end lines up in a wide 6 alignment, and the weakside linebacker lines up in a 6 alignment behind the line of scrimmage. On running plays designed to go to the strongside, the weakside defensive end is responsible for the reverse and the weakside linebacker is responsible for cutbacks in the B gap.

4-3 Gap Responsibilities—Strongside Run

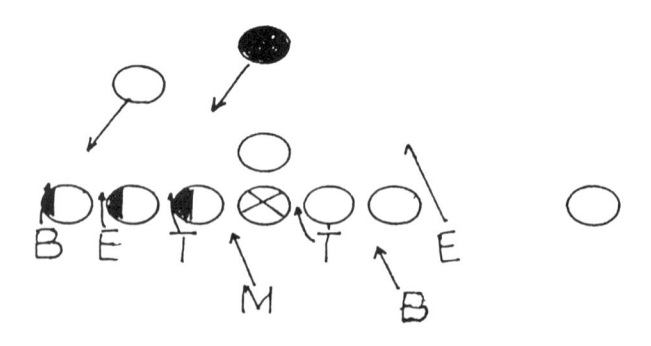

STRONGSIDE END—C Gap - Squeeze B Gap.
WEAKSIDE END—Contain reverse.
STRONGSIDE TACKLE—B gap - Squeeze A gap.
WEAKSIDE TACKLE—A gap.
MIDDLE LINEBACKER—Strongside A gap to the ball.
STRONGSIDE LINEBACKER—Force or cutback depending on coverage.
WEAKSIDE LINEBACKER—B gap.

BASIC FRONTS 47

4-3 Gap Responsibilities—Weakside Run

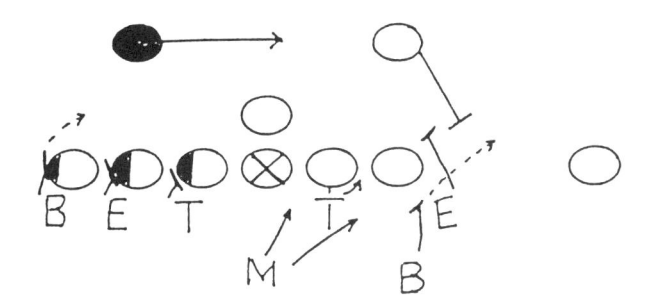

STRONGSIDE END—C gap - Squeeze B gap.
WEAKSIDE END—Force or cutback depending on coverage.
STRONGSIDE TACKLE—B gap - Squeeze A gap.
WEAKSIDE TACKLE—B gap.
MIDDLE LINEBACKER—Weakside A gap to the ball.
STRONGSIDE LINEBACKER—Squeeze C gap - Reverse.
WEAKSIDE LINEBACKER—Block out by tackle, keep all blockers on inside pad and squeeze—all other weakside runs downhill, inside-out to the ball.

THE 4-3 VERSUS WEAKSIDE RUN FORMATIONS

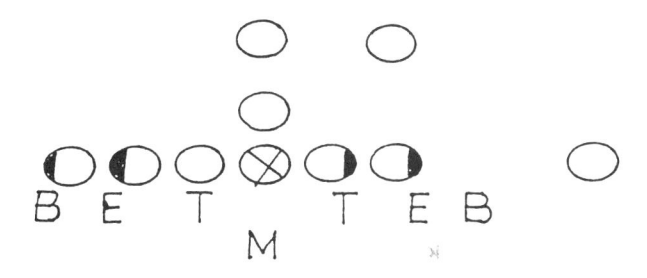

Versus formations where the run strength is to the weakside, the tackles adjust their alignments to that side. That is, the weakside tackle lines up in a 3 alignment and the strongside tackle in a 2 alignment.

The weakside end lines up in a tight 6 alignment and is responsible for squeezing the B gap on running plays designed to go to the strongside of the formation. The weakside linebacker lines up about one and one-half yards outside the defensive end on the line of scrimmage. On strongside runs, he is responsible for the reverse. A change-up call can be made from this alignment that involves the defensive end and linebacker exchanging responsibilities on strongside runs. That is, even though they line up in the weakside adjustment, the end in a tight 6 alignment is responsible for the reverse, and the outside linebacker is responsible to slide behind the line and take all cutbacks in the weakside B gap. The exchanging of responsibilities on strongside runs is merely a change up. I do not believe it should be used on every down due to the fact that if the offense can count on this type of gap responsibility, types of blocking schemes can be utilized that make the defense vulnerable to cutbacks in the B gap.

4-3 Gap Responsibilities—Strongside Run

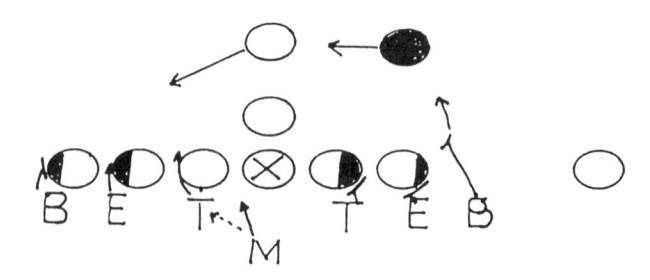

BASIC FRONTS 49

4-3 Gap Responsibilities—Strongside Run—With Change Up Or Exchange Call Between Weakside End and Weakside Linebacker

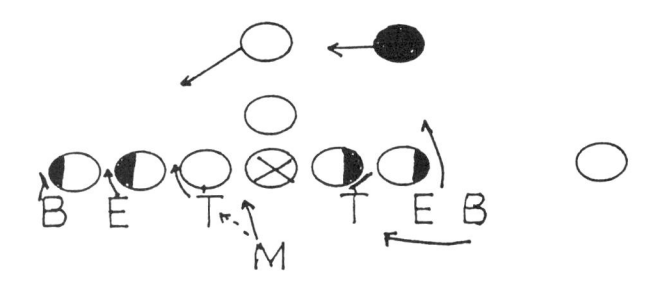

STRONGSIDE END—C gap - Squeeze B gap.
WEAKSIDE END—Squeeze B gap - Exchange call - Contain - Reverse.
STRONGSIDE TACKLE—B gap.
WEAKSIDE TACKLE—Squeeze B gap.
MIDDLE LINEBACKER—Strongside A gap to the ball.
STRONGSIDE LINEBACKER—Force or cutback depending on coverage called.
WEAKSIDE LINEBACKER—Contain - Reverse unless exchange call is used, then weakside B gap (cutback).

Run-Gap Responsibilities When the Defense Is Adjusted to Weakside Running Formations: 4-3 Gap Responsibilities—Weakside Run

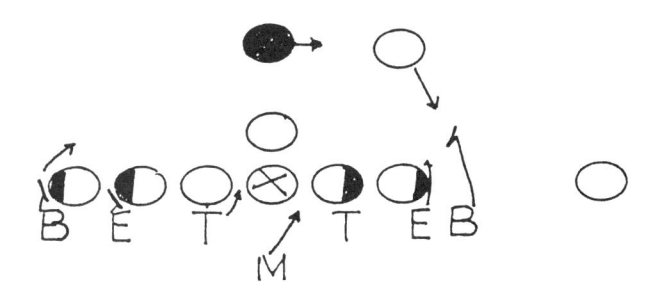

STRONGSIDE END—C gap - Squeeze B gap.
WEAKSIDE END—C gap - Squeeze B gap.
STRONGSIDE TACKLE—A gap.
WEAKSIDE TACKLE—B gap.
MIDDLE LINEBACKER—Weakside A gap to the ball.
STRONGSIDE LINEBACKER—Squeeze C gap - Reverse.
WEAKSIDE LINEBACKER—Force or cutback depending on coverage called.

THE 4-3 VERSUS BALANCED FORMATIONS

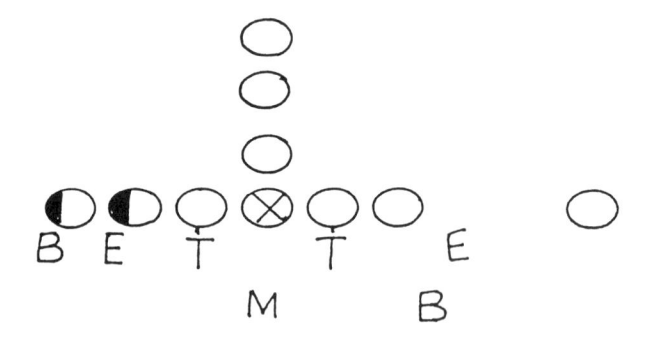

Versus formations that are balanced in their ability to attack the weakside and strongside of the defense effectively, both tackles are lined up in a 2 alignment. An example of this type of formation is the "I." With this type of offensive deployment, the fullback is available to be used as a lead blocker with equal effectiveness to either side of the formation.

The utilization of a 2 alignment by both tackles means that they are both two gappers. That is, they line up head up on the guards, and they are responsible for either the A or B gap to their side of the formation. For example: On running plays designed to attack the strongside of the formation, the strongside tackle is responsible for the strongside B gap. On running plays designed to attack the weakside of the formation, he is responsible for the strongside A gap. The general rule for both tackles is: Run his way, he is responsible for the B gap; run to the opposite side of the formation, he has the A gap his side.

4-3 2 Alignment—Tackle Gap Responsibility Versus Strongside Run

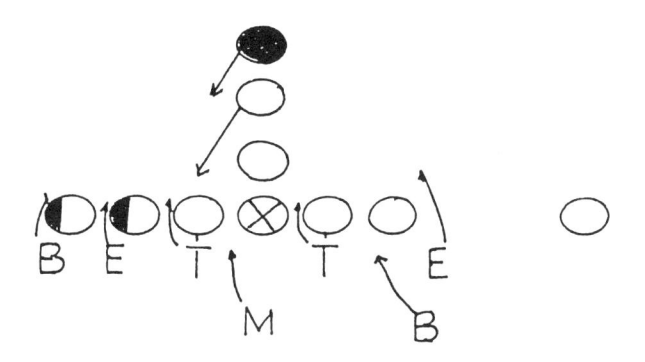

4-3 2 Alignment—Tackle Gap Responsibility Versus Weakside Run

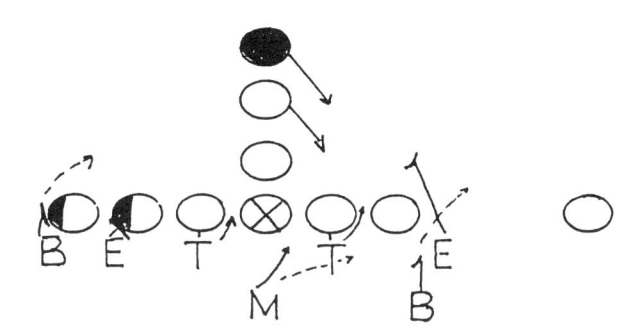

The alignments and responsibilities of the middle linebacker, strongside linebacker and strongside defensive end are not affected by these types of formations. The most effective way to use the weakside defensive end and linebacker against these types of formations is to utilize the stacked adjustment. That is, the defensive end lines up in a wide 6 alignment, and the weakside linebacker lines up in a 6 off the ball behind the line of scrimmage.

4-3 DEFENSE VERSUS TWO TIGHT ENDS

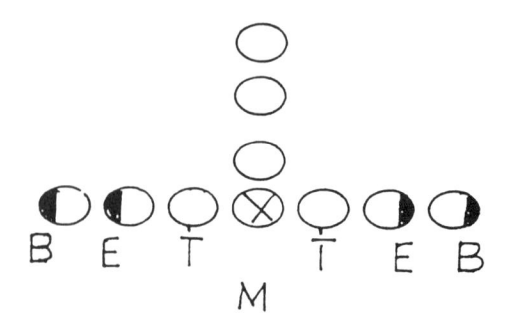

The 4-3 defense adjusts very well to offensive formations that utilize multiple tight ends. If the second tight end lines up on the line of scrimmage, the weakside defensive end and linebacker line up in exactly the same alignments they use as strongside players. They assume the same gap responsibilities they have as strongside players. That is, on runs designed to attack their side, the defensive end is a C gap player, and the linebacker is either a force man or he is responsible for cutback if a corner or safety is responsible for force outside him. On runs designed to go to the strongside, the weakside defensive end is responsible to squeeze the B gap and defend the C gap. On plays away, the weakside linebacker has the responsibility of squeezing the C gap as well as defending the reverse.

4-3 STACK DEFENSE

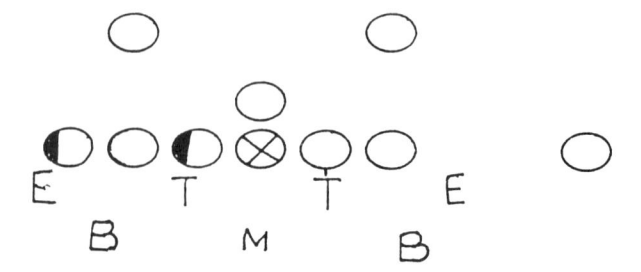

BASIC FRONTS

The 4-3 Stack Defense involves both defensive ends lining up as outside players on the line of scrimmage. If there is a tight end to their side of the formation, the defensive ends line up in a tight 9 alignment. If there is no tight end to their side, the defensive ends line up in a wide 6 alignment.

The strongside and weakside outside linebackers line up in 6 alignments three yards to three and one-half yards off the line of scrimmage.

The defensive tackles make the same adjustments in their alignments as they do in a 4-3 defense versus the various formations.

The middle linebacker's alignment and responsibilities are the same as they are in a 4-3 defense.

The value of this defense is that it is perfectly balanced because both sides of the defense are the same. The defensive ends are always outside players, and the strongside and weakside linebackers are inside players lined up over the offensive tackles.

Another advantage of this defense is that the defensive ends should, by their alignment, be in a position to defeat the tight ends. I have always felt that a defensive end should consistently defeat a tight end who is trying to block him on run or pass plays. The linebackers, although they usually are smaller than the tackles, almost always are quicker and more athletic and can make plays because of their athleticism. Their alignment behind the line of scrimmage and off the ball allows them to make plays on both sides of the formation. Conversely, when linebackers are aligned on the line of scrimmage, as they are in the 4-3 defense, they are pretty much limited to making plays on runs to their side of the line of scrimmage.

4-3 Stack Gap Responsibilities—Strongside Run

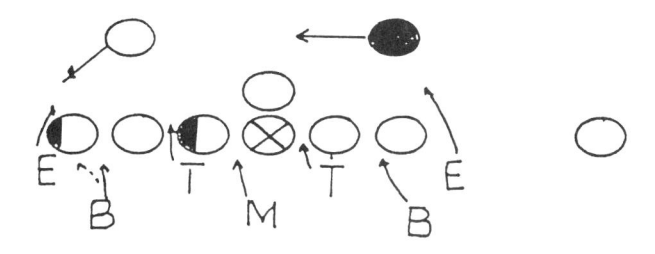

STRONGSIDE END—Force or cutback depending on coverage.
WEAKSIDE END—Contain reverse - Squeeze B gap.
STRONGSIDE TACKLE—B gap strongside.
WEAKSIDE TACKLE—A gap weakside.
MIDDLE LINEBACKER—Strongside A gap to the ball.
STRONGSIDE LINEBACKER—C gap to the ball.
WEAKSIDE LINEBACKER—B gap weakside.

4-3 Stack Gap Responsibilities—Weakside Runs

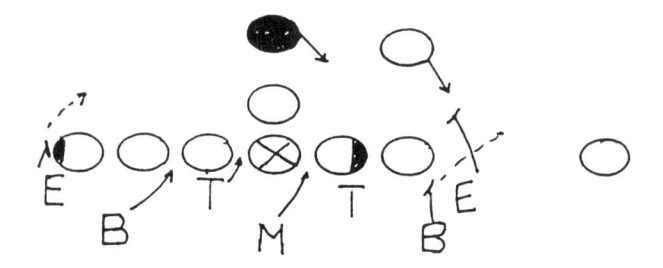

STRONGSIDE END—Contain reverse - Squeeze C gap.
WEAKSIDE END—Force or cutback depending on coverage.
STRONGSIDE TACKLE—Strongside A gap.
WEAKSIDE TACKLE—Weakside B gap.
MIDDLE LINEBACKER—Weakside A gap to the ball.
STRONGSIDE LINEBACKER—Strongside B gap to the ball.
WEAKSIDE LINEBACKER—Tackle blocks out. Keep ball and all blockers on inside pad and squeeze—all other weakside runs downhill and inside-out to the ball.

4-3 UNDER DEFENSE

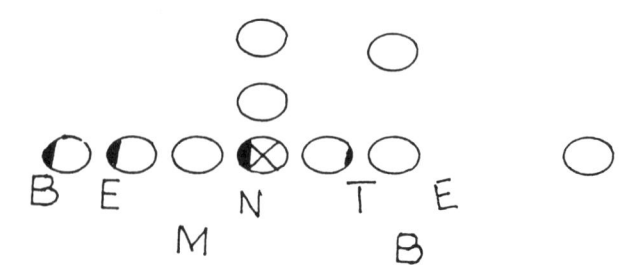

BASIC FRONTS

The alignments of the defensive linemen in the under defense are not affected by the run strength of formations. The nose tackle aligns in an O strong alignment. That is, he lines up with his inside eye looking through the near shoulder of the center into the core of the backfield. The defensive tackle lines up in a 3 alignment on the weakside, or open side, of the formation.

The strongside defensive end lines up in a 6 alignment, and the weakside defensive end aligns in a wide 6.

4-3 Under Gap Responsibilities—Strongside Run

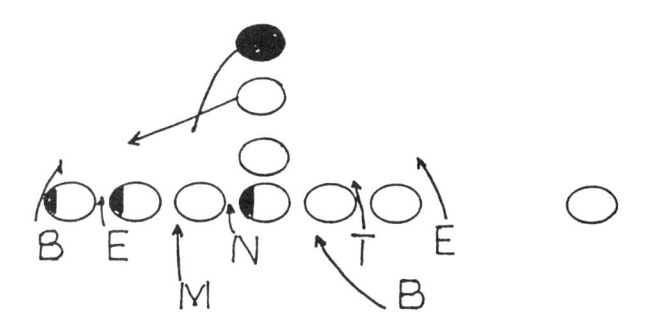

NOSE TACKLE—Strongside A Gap.
WEAKSIDE TACKLE—B gap - Squeeze A gap.
STRONGSIDE END—C gap - Squeeze B gap.
WEAKSIDE END—Contain reverse - Squeeze B gap.
MIDDLE LINEBACKER—B gap to the ball.
STRONGSIDE LINEBACKER—Force or cutback depending on coverage.
WEAKSIDE LINEBACKER—Weakside A gap.

4-3 Under Gap Responsibilities—Weakside Runs

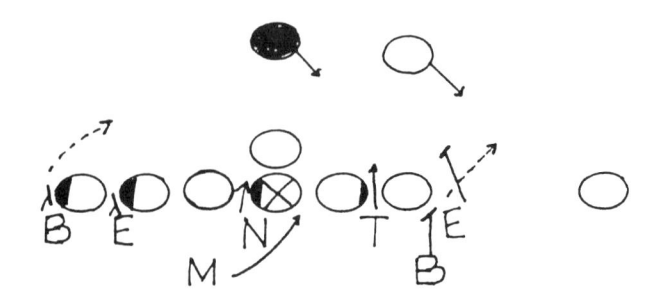

NOSE TACKLE—Strongside A gap - Squeeze weakside A gap.
WEAKSIDE TACKLE—B gap.
STRONGSIDE END—C gap - Squeeze B gap.
WEAKSIDE END—Force or cutback depending on coverage.
MIDDLE LINEBACKER—Weakside A gap.
STRONGSIDE LINEBACKER—Squeeze C gap - Reverse.
WEAKSIDE LINEBACKER—Block out by tackle. Keep all blockers on inside pad and squeeze—all weakside runs downhill and inside-out to the ball.

4-3 OVER DEFENSE

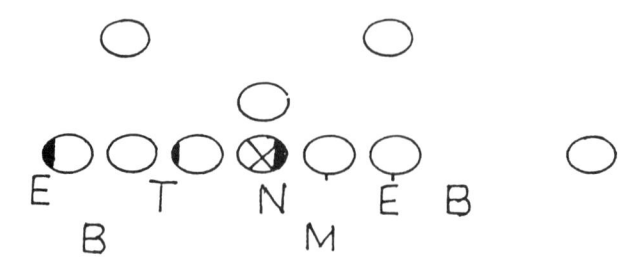

The most important advantage the over defense has over other types of alignments is the matchup of a defensive end lining up over a tight end. As mentioned earlier, this matchup should favor the defense. A defensive end should always win the one-on-one confrontation with a tight end on both running and passing plays.

The nose tackle lines up in an O weak alignment. The strongside tackle lines up in a 3 alignment. The strongside defensive end lines up in a 9 alignment over the tight end. The normal or base alignment of the weakside defensive end is a 5. However, he may line up in a 6 whenever the weakside outside linebacker stacks behind the line. This change-up of alignments and assignments between the weakside defensive end and the outside linebacker may be used versus formations whose primary run strength is to the strongside. Strong formations and trips formations would be examples of these types of formations.

4-3 Over Gap Responsibilities—Strongside Run

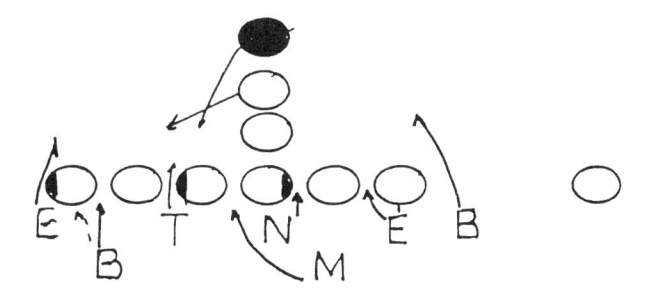

4-3 Over Gap Responsibilities—Strongside Runs—With Weakside Change-up Alignment

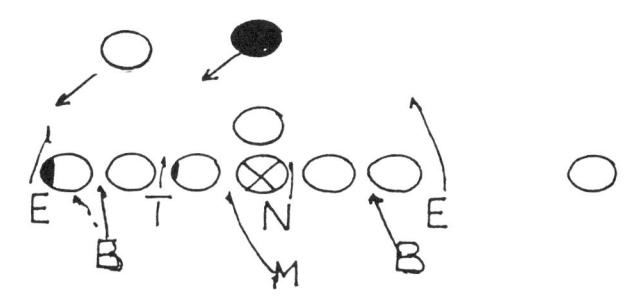

NOSE TACKLE—Weakside A gap - Squeeze strongside A.
STRONGSIDE TACKLE—B gap.

STRONGSIDE END—Force or cutback depending on coverage.
WEAKSIDE END—Base alignment - B gap.
Change-up alignment 6 - Contain reverse - Squeeze B gap.
MIDDLE LINEBACKER—Strongside A gap.
STRONGSIDE LINEBACKER—C gap to the ball.
WEAKSIDE LINEBACKER—Base alignment on L.O.S. - Contain reverse.
Change-up alignment 5 behind L.O.S. - B gap.

4-3 Over Gap Responsibilities—Weakside Run

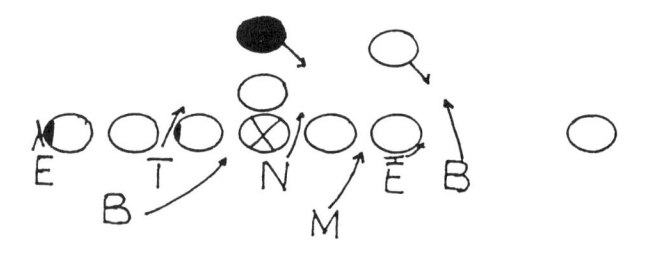

NOSE TACKLE—Weakside A gap.
STRONGSIDE TACKLE—B gap - Squeeze A gap.
STRONGSIDE END—Contain reverse - Squeeze C gap.
WEAKSIDE END—5 alignment C gap - Change-up alignment - Cutback or force depending on coverge called.
MIDDLE LINEBACKER—Weakside B gap to the ball.
STRONGSIDE LINEBACKER—Strongside A gap to the ball.
WEAKSIDE LINEBACKER—Base alignment on L.O.S. - Force or cutback depending on coverage.
Change-up alignment - Block out by tackle. Keep all blockers on inside pad and squeeze—all weakside runs downhill and inside-out to the ball.

The over and under defenses are good examples of how flexibility in alignments can be accomplished with relative ease. For example: Once a defensive tackle learns how to play a 3 technique on the left side as well as the right, he is now ready to play the 3 alignment tackle in both the over and under defenses. The same is true for the nose—after learning the offset nose position on both sides, he now is ready to play both the under and over defenses.

3-4 DEFENSE

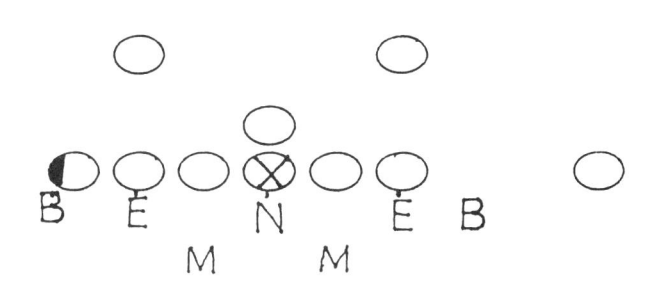

```
          O         O
              O
   O  O  O  ⊗  O  O
   B  E     N     E  B         O
          M     M
```

The nose tackle in the 3-4 defense lines up in an O alignment or head up on the offensive center. From this alignment he is a two-gap player. That is, he is responsible for the A gap to the side of the formation the running play is designed to attack.

The defensive ends can line up in either a 5 or a 6 alignment. If they line up in a 5, they are two-gap players. That is, on plays designed to attack their side of the formation they are responsible for the C gap. On plays to the opposite side of the formation they are responsible for the B gap.

If they line up in a 6, their responsibility on plays designed to attack their side of the formation is the same as it is if they line up in a 5; that is, the C gap. However, on plays to the opposite side of the formation their responsibility is different. On these types of plays, rather than putting their body in the B gap as they do when they are in a 5, they squeeze the B gap with the body of the blocker.

The two-gap or 5 alignment by the ends is, in my opinion, the best way to play the 3-4 defense. When the defensive ends use a 5 alignment, their responsibilities can be described very simply. Their job is to knock the offensive tackle back and play the C gap on plays their way and the B gap on plays away. Of these two responsibilities knocking the tackle back is the most important. The knocking-back of the tackle allows the linebacker playing behind the defensive end to play downhill, or toward the line of scrimmage. In the event the defensive end does get reach-blocked, the linebacker can easily adjust his gap responsibility and defend the C gap on wide plays to his side of the formation. The primary reason I prefer the 5 technique is that it is much more difficult for an offensive lineman to block a defensive lineman, who uses his hands well, in the head-up position than it is to block a shaded player or one lined up in a gap.

3-4 Defense Gap Responsibilities—Strongside Run

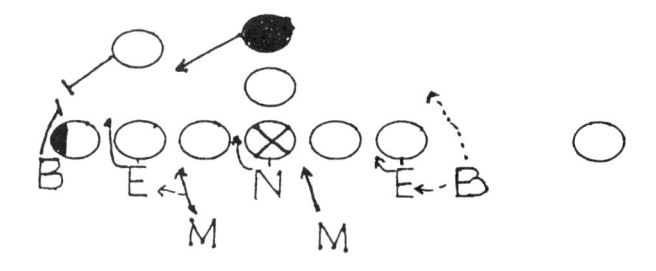

NOSE—A gap strongside.
STRONGSIDE END—C gap - 5 or 6 alignment.
WEAKSIDE END—B gap.
STRONGSIDE OUTSIDE LINEBACKER—Force or cutback depending on coverage.
WEAKSIDE OUTSIDE LINEBACKER—Contain - Reverse.
STRONGSIDE INSIDE LINEBACKER—B gap to C gap to the ball on wide runs.
WEAKSIDE INSIDE LINEBACKER—Weakside A gap.

3-4 Defense Gap Responsibilities—Weakside Runs

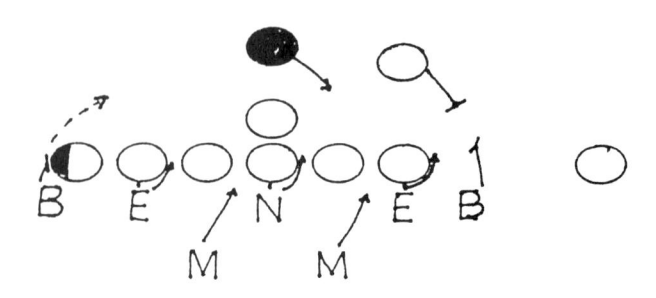

NOSE—A gap weakside.
STRONGSIDE END—5 alignment B gap - 6 alignment squeeze B gap.
WEAKSIDE END—C gap.
STRONGSIDE OUTSIDE LINEBACKER—Squeeze C gap - Reverse.
WEAKSIDE OUTSIDE LINEBACKER—Force or cutback depending on coverage.
STRONGSIDE INSIDE LINEBACKER—A gap strongside.
WEAKSIDE INSIDE LINEBACKER—B gap to C gap to the ball on wide runs.

46 DEFENSE

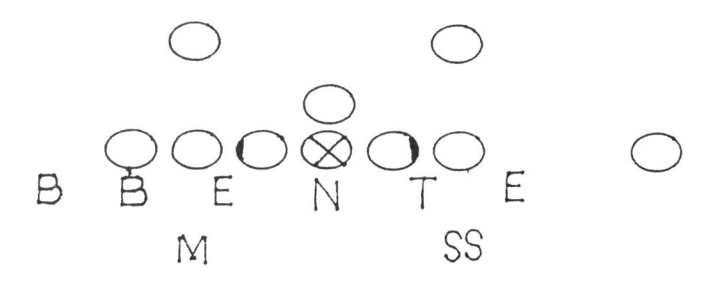

```
       O           O
            O
     O O O⊗O O          O
   B  B  E  N  T  E
      M           SS
```

All the defensive alignments discussed to this point have been seven-man fronts. That is, there are seven men in various combinations of linemen and linebackers who line up within five yards of the line of scrimmage. The 46 defense is an eight-man front. The additional player is a safety who lines up within five yards of the line of scrimmage. Although there are many variations of this alignment, the most popular utilizes four linemen, three linebackers and four defensive backs. When I coached at the Los Angeles Rams, we developed a version of this alignment that utilized only two linemen, replacing the third and fourth linemen with linebackers. We called this defense the Eagle Five-Linebacker Defense because the personnel involved consisted of five linebackers, two defensive linemen and four defensive backs.

This defense is characterized by two players lining up in a wide 3 alignment. The strongside end and the weakside tackle are the players who are lined up in a 3. They are aggressive, penetrating players in the B gap. They key the guards and react to blocks by the tackles.

The other tackle lines up in an O alignment. He is a knock-'em-back, two-gap player. The weakside defensive end lines up in a wide 6 alignment. In this defense the players can flop. That is, they can be designated strongside or weakside ends or tackles and line up and execute their responsibilities (a) to the tight-end side if they are strongside players or (b) away from the tight end if they are weakside players. If this method of personnel deployment were not used, the ends would have to learn to play a strongside 3 and a weakside wide 6 alignment. The tackles would have to learn how to play an O and a weakside 3 alignment. For simplicity's sake, it is much easier to flop the linemen so that the nose is always a nose, the other tackle always plays a 3 alignment, and the ends play either a weakside or wide 6 or a strongside 3.

46 Defense Gap Responsibilities—Strongside Run

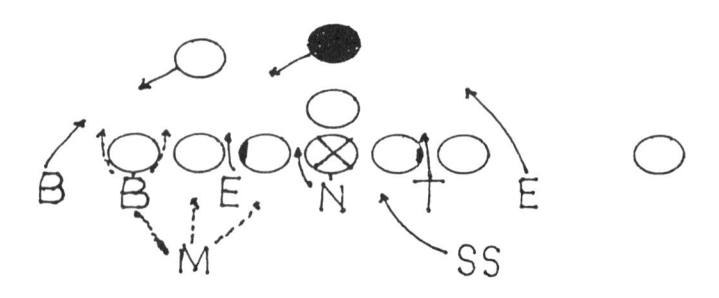

STRONGSIDE END—B gap - Penetrate.
WEAKSIDE END—Chase - Contain reverse.
NOSE TACKLE—A gap strongside.
WEAKSIDE TACKLE—B gap - Squeeze A gap.
OUTSIDE LINEBACKER—Force - Contain wide run.
LINEBACKER OVER TIGHT END—C gap run inside - D gap or cutback wide run.
MIDDLE LINEBACKER—Strongside A gap any run designed to attack strongside A or B gap—C gap to D gap to the ball on strongside wide runs.
STRONG SAFETY—Weakside A gap.

46 Defense Gap Responsibilities—Weakside Run

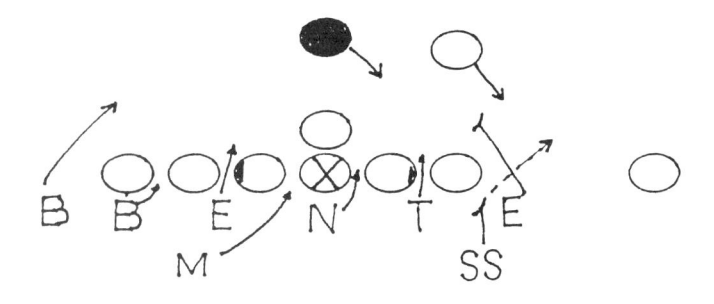

STRONGSIDE END—B gap - Squeeze A gap.
WEAKSIDE END—Hold C gap and squeeze on any base block on the end by the offensive tackle. Any other block close and two gap - Bounce wide play deep.
NOSE TACKLE—A gap weakside.
WEAKSIDE TACKLE—B gap.
OUTSIDE LINEBACKER—Chase - Contain reverse.
LINEBACKER OVER TIGHT END—C gap.
MIDDLE LINEBACKER—A gap strongside to the ball.
STRONG SAFETY—Base block by the offensive tackle on weakside defensive end; step up and keep all blockers and the ball on your inside shoulder pad. Any other block, play inside-out toward the line of scrimmage to the ball.

SUMMARY

This chapter covered the defensive front alignments most used in all levels of football today. After defensive linemen have learned how to play the various alignments, they are prepared to play any defensive scheme you choose to use. This method of teaching numbered alignments, gap responsibilities, keys and reads gives you unlimited possibilities for flexibility in your defensive scheme.

7

Rushing the Passer

The ability to rush the passer is characteristic of all good defensive linemen. Rushing the passer is an art that requires constant work and attention to detail. Although great pass rushers usually possess superior athletic skills, especially those of speed and quickness, less gifted athletes can develop into effective players in this area. As with any other phase of defensive line play, players can be taught to rush the passer effectively regardless of their level of athleticism.

OBJECTIVES OF THE RUSHER

Obviously, the primary objective of the pass rusher is to tackle the quarterback before he throws the ball. The tackling, or sacking, of the quarterback is a huge defensive play that usually results in a sizable loss of yardage and has a devastating effect on an offensive team in a series of downs. The momentum of many football games has been changed by the quarterback sack. Since pass offenses are so dependent upon a rhythm being established between the quarterback and his receivers, the sack, like no other play, creates uncertainty and therefore a disruption of this coordinated effort.

Rushing the passer is one place in defensive football where being close counts. In other words, a defensive player does not always need to sack the quarterback to be effective as a rusher. For example: A player rushing the quarterback can have a very real effect on the passer by being in front of him, in his sight line, with hands up.

Next to the sack, the most positive effect a rusher can have is to deflect a thrown ball. This deflecting of the ball means that the pass does not have to be defended by pass defenders down the field. In other words, there is no chance for the offense to complete a pass when it is deflected behind the line. The other positive effect of a deflected ball is that the defense can intercept the ball, creating a turnover.

In addition to the sack and the deflected ball, the rusher in front of the quarterback, in his sight line with his hands up, can force the passer to throw the ball over his hands, thereby forcing a high trajectory. The more the passer is forced to throw over the hands, the higher the arc of the ball, which relates to more reaction time for the secondary to make a play on the ball.

In addition, the rusher's uplifted hands often have the effect of obstructing the passer's vision so that the quarterback either does not see receivers who are open or misjudges the throw he makes to one of them.

In front of the passer, in his sight line, is without question the most desirable place for a pass rusher to be in order to affect the passer's accuracy. I really believe a rusher is more effective five yards away from the passer, in front of him, than he is a yard away but out of his sight line. However, a good hit on the passer, when he doesn't see it coming, can also be very effective. These blindside hits often result in fumbles and changes of possession that decide games. Even if these types of hits do not result in fumbles, they do have an effect on the passer. After being hit from the blind side, many passers become nervous and lose their effectiveness.

Pressure on the passer can have the effect of causing him to pull the ball down and run with it. There are many accurate passers who are limited as quarterback runners, and it's this kind of quarterback a defensive team would like to get to pull the ball down with its constant pressure.

At any level of football, good pass defense starts with a good pass rush. I happen to be one who believes that, given enough time, most passers can be effective. By the same token, even the best passers lose their effectiveness when hurried by the pass rush.

FUNDAMENTALS OF THE PASS RUSH

Takeoff

Takeoff is best described as the forward movement of a defensive player triggered by the movement of an offensive player or the ball. The alignment of the defensive player must allow him to see the man he is lined up over as well as the ball. In most cases the ball will be the first thing that moves on the offensive side of the line of scrimmage. However, some offensive players will occasionally jump the count or move before the ball is snapped. This split-second pre-snap movement by the offensive man is used to give him an advantage. It gives him additional time to set up and to prepare for the charge of the defensive player. The general rule is that the defensive player's takeoff is initiated or ignited by the movement of an offensive man or the ball, whichever moves first.

Elevation

In most cases the offensive pass blocker is trying to establish a new line of scrimmage. That is, he retreats or sets back on drop-back pass plays to increase the distance between him and the defensive player. This setting up, or setting back, has, as its purpose, the buying of time to establish a blocking position and move in front of the pass rusher. Takeoff has, as its primary purpose, the reducing of this pass-set time. Therefore, the quicker the defender can engage, or make contact with the pass blocker, the more effective he will be in rushing the passer.

Good pass-rush technique involves the rusher quickly gaining as much ground as he can toward the offensive side of the ball or across the line of scrimmage. The lower he is in his initial takeoff the more ground he will gain toward the passer. If, on the other hand, he raises up out of his stance, he will be slowed in his ability to engage or pressure the pass blocker.

Another aspect of good elevation or low body trajectory on takeoff is that it allows the rusher to have a leverage advantage when he engages the pass protector. As is the case in defeating run blockers, the player whose shoulder level or face mask is lower than that of his opponent usually wins the one-on-one battles with respect to leverage.

STRAIGHT LINES

It is important that pass rushers understand that the shortest route to the passer is a straight line. That is, the old geometrical axiom that says the shortest distance between two points is a straight line applies here. The relationship or angle in which the rusher aligns, as it relates to the line of scrimmage, is important here. For example: A defensive end lined up in a wide 6 alignment on the line of scrimmage should align at an angle with the line of scrimmage. That is, he should be turned in, or cocked, in his stance so that his initial steps point him in a straight-line path to the point where he anticipates the passer will be when the ball is thrown. Too many times wide-aligned rushers line up square in their stance or with their shoulders parallel with the line of scrimmage. When they do, they waste a lot of time and lengthen their route to the passer by taking a straight-up-the-field course and then having to adjust their course to turn to the passer during the pass rush down.

In addition to the stance, the straight-line aspect of the pass rush is important because it applies to other principles involved in the rush technique. That is, for example, that the shortest route to the passer for an inside pass rusher like a defensive tackle is over or through the position occupied by the offensive guard trying to block him—although *quick* moves around blockers can be effective. The most effective pass-rush techniques involve straight-line or short routes to the passer.

This is best accomplished by teaching techniques that emphasize the upfield aspect of the pass rush.

FEET

The ability of the pass rusher to move his feet quickly and change directions is one big factor that determines how effective a defensive lineman can be in this area. Almost all the actions of the feet in the pass rush will consist of short, choppy steps. In fact, the only time the pass rusher should use long strides is when he sprints to engage the blocker or as he sprints by him on the pass-rush move.

It is very important for the rusher to think in terms of his toes always pointing toward the passer all the way through the pass rush down. This starts with his stance and continues through the finish of the pass rush. A great example of the toes pointing toward the quarterback is the defensive end when he is making a hard outside pass-rush charge. As the rusher rushes up the field, the tackle will try to push the defensive end upfield by the passer as he steps up. If the rusher continues with his toes pointed upfield, he will be pushed upfield by the passer. If, however, the rusher corrects his angle and points his toes toward the passer or toward the line of scrimmage, he has a chance to have an effect on the passer with his rush.

The feet are an essential part of the pass-rush technique. Pass rushers who can play with their feet under them are always under control. This allows them to change directions quickly and to effectively react to pass-related plays like draws and screens and to use power and leverage when it is required in the pass rush.

HANDS

Rushing the passer requires that the pass rusher be good at using his hands. Every pass-rush technique demands that the hands of the rusher be used as effective tools. The hands are used to power through the pass blocker or turn him. The ideal position for the pass-rusher's hands, if he is trying to power rush a pass blocker, is the outside upper tips of the front numbers on his jersey. The hands must be driven inside-out toward the upper tips of the front numbers. Since the offensive pass blocker is trying to use his hands to strike the front numbers of the rusher, it is imperative that the defensive player be the one with his hands inside.

Power rushing requires that both hands of the rusher be inside under the shoulder pads of the blocker. On all other types of pass-rush moves, only one hand of the rusher need be inside. The other hand, often called the off hand or arm, is used to push, pull, club or in some way turn the blocker as the rusher goes by him.

In addition to striking, pushing or driving the hands as part of the pass-rush technique, the ability to grab the blocker is also essential. The combination of pushing with one hand and grabbing with the other is one of the techniques most commonly used in rushing the passer. This combination of the simultaneous pushing, pulling and therefore turning of the blocker is designed to compromise the pass blocker's parallel relationship with the line of scrimmage. The objective is to open a straight-line lane to the passer by turning the blocker. A pass blocker who is able to maintain a position with his hips and shoulders parallel with the line of scrimmage, as he is blocking, takes up a lot of area. He makes it very difficult to get to the passer quickly. In other words, he has created a long route to the passer. By turning the blocker, the rusher shortens the route by decreasing the area the pass protector occupies. Again, rather than having to go around the blocker, the rusher moves toward the passer through part of the area that was occupied by the blocker!

HEAD-UP CORNER, OR EDGE, OF THE BLOCKER

Head Up

As we have mentioned previously, the shortest and quickest distance to the passer is a straight line. With that in mind, there are a number of important principles to consider. One is that when a rusher is aligned head up on a pass protector, his shortest route to the passer is a straight line over and through the blocker. In most cases a rusher attempting to rush in this fashion will leverage or power rush the pass blocker. That is, he will either drive the blocker back and deposit him in the lap of the passer or he will run through the blocker, deposit him on his back and proceed to the passer. Another option a head-up rusher has is to start a power rush on the blocker, throw him out of his path and proceed to the passer.

In addition to the forms of power rushing described above, the pass rusher who lines up head up has other, sometimes more desirable, options. The most effective alignment from which to rush the passer is on the corner, edge, or shade, on the pass blocker. Therefore, the rusher who lines up head up is at a disadvantage if he is not able to power rush through the blocker or throw him out of the lane. If the head-up-aligned pass rusher does not elect to power rush, he must, as quickly as possible after he recognizes pass, work to the edge, or corner, of the blocker; that is, establish a pass-rush lane over the inside or outside shoulder of the lineman he is lined up over.

Corner, or Edge, of the Blocker

The most advantageous alignment a pass rusher can use is some type of outside shade; that is, an alignment that puts him on the outside eye or outside shoulder of the pass blocker he lines up over. The defensive player's inside eye is looking through the offensive player's outside eye or outside shoulder into the core of the backfield. Defensive ends who play on the open side of the formation, or away from the tight end whenever the scheme allows, very often line up as much as one and one-half yards outside the offensive tackle.

The obvious advantage the various shade alignments have is that the position the pass rusher lines up in places him on the corner of a blocker. Whereas, from the head-up position the rusher must work to the corner, or edge, of the blocker after he has diagnosed the play as a pass. This, of course, has the effect of delaying the actual pass-rush technique employed by the rusher.

The edge, or corner, of the blocker is desirable as the best path to the passer for several reasons. One is that the corner, or edge, of the blocker represents a shorter straight-line path to the passer. As was previously discussed, the head-up position means the rusher has a more challenging, longer route to the passer. Another very important advantage of rushing over the corner of the blocker is that the wider alignment usually causes the pass blocker to compromise his squared-up, or parallel, relationship with the line of scrimmage. When this turning happens, it usually has the effect of making the pass blocker more vulnerable to straight-line rushes outside and counter-moves inside.

One advantage of the head-up alignment is that it does allow the defender to better read and react to pass-related plays such as draws. When a player shades, he has a tendency to rush upfield and be pushed by these types of plays by the pass protector. Since the key to reacting to these types of plays is the defensive player's ability to maintain a squared-up position with his hips and shoulders parallel with the line of scrimmage, the head-up pass rusher has an advantage here. As soon as the shaded rusher reads a draw play, he must avoid being pushed up the field and work to square his hips and shoulders with the line of scrimmage. He should drive his inside hand to the inside number on the front of the jersey of the blocker who is trying to block him. This squaring-up process allows the pass rusher to squeeze, or compress, the running lane the offense is trying to create.

PHASES OF THE PASS RUSH

Stance

The most effective pass-rush stance for shaded players is an elongated stance with hips high and a considerable amount of weight on the hand on the ground. Players who align head up should be in a more balanced or bunched stance with their body weight distributed equally between their feet and the hand they have on the ground. In this type of stance the player's back will be parallel with the ground, with the hips slightly lower than the shoulders.

Get Off on Movement (Takeoff)

Pass rush starts with takeoff. Takeoff is the reaction by a pass rusher to movement that occurs on the line of scrimmage. On movement by the offensive blocker or the ball, the rusher attempts to cross the line of scrimmage as quickly as he can. The objective for the defensive player is to pressure the pass blocker as quickly as he can after movement occurs by the offense. It is important that the takeoff by the pass rusher be low and hard and that he not raise up out of his stance. His shoulder level should not change out of his stance. This ensures that most of the rusher's movement will be across the line of scrimmage, not up.

Engage the Blocker

With his initial takeoff the pass rusher should sprint to the blocker. His hands should be driven to engage the blocker at the outside tips of the blocker's front numbers or under his shoulder pads. The quicker the rusher can engage the pass blocker, the better. It is important for the rusher to remember that the pass blocker is setting back or establishing a new line of scrimmage. He is doing this to give him time to pass set and prepare to block the onrushing lineman. He is also setting back in order to read the type of charge the rusher is using. In addition, it is better to pick up pass-rush games and stunts from this pass-set position than on the line of scrimmage.

It is very important that the pass rusher have a leverage advantage over the pass blocker as he engages him. Low, hard takeoff is a good start toward the pass rusher having a leverage advantage over the pass blocker. A good point of reference in this regard is the face mask or shoulder level of the rusher. If his face mask or shoulder level is lower than that of the pass blocker, the rusher will usually have a leverage advantage.

It is also important for the rusher to have his feet under him as he engages the blocker. Even though he reaches to power, push or pull the blocker, the rusher needs to have his weight distributed over his feet in order to quickly change direction throughout the execution of pass-rush techniques.

Power or Work to the Corner of the Blocker

As the pass rusher engages the pass blocker, he will either power rush or work to the corner of the blocker. If he power rushes, he will strike with his hand through the blocker's front numbers and either drive him into the passer or throw the blocker out of his rush lane and proceed to the quarterback.

If he does not power rush, the rusher will work to the corner, or edge, of the blocker. The objective here is to establish the shortest possible course or lane to the quarterback.

Turn the Blocker

Most pass-rush moves are some combination of push, pull or turn the blocker. These rush techniques are designed to compromise the pass protector's parallel relationship with the line of scrimmage. By maintaining a position with his hips and shoulders parallel with the line of scrimmage, the pass blocker occupies a large area and thereby creates a long route around him to the passer. By turning the blocker, the rusher shortens his route to the passer. The objective here is for the rusher to rush in his designated lane and get the blocker out of it.

Keep the Feet Moving or Working

The feet of the pass rusher should be working or moving throughout the pass-rush move. The quick-feet movement of the rusher enables him to change directions quickly. The foot movement of the pass rusher is characterized by short, choppy six-inch steps. The only big steps or long strides are the initial steps as the rusher takes off out of his stance or as he accelerates by the pass blocker on the pass-rush move.

Make a Pass-Rush Move by the Blocker

With the hands and feet moving in a coordinated effort the pass rusher should make a pass-rush move toward the passer. As the rusher turns or throws the pass blocker out of his rush lane, he should accelerate by the blocker. Again, this is where the rusher should use long strides or sprint past the blocker. He must accelerate past the blocker to avoid giving the pass protector time to recover.

Keep the Eyes Focused on the Passer

It is important that the pass rusher see the passer all the way through the execution of pass-rush techniques. He should look through the blocker to the passer. Focusing on the passer allows the rusher to change his course and move in front of the quarterback in the passing lane. Seeing the quarterback will also allow the rusher to raise his hands as the passer begins his passing motion.

Get in Passer's Throwing Lane

The passer will always want to have an open, unobstructed lane in the direction he wants to throw the ball. The pass rusher is most effective when he appears as an obstruction in the passing lane. The pass rusher can have an effect on the pass play even though he may be a considerable distance from the passer but in front of him.

There are times when a pass rusher breaks free at a point where the quarterback does not see him. When this occurs and the rusher has the opportunity to sack the quarterback, he should do it with great velocity. These blindside, big hits can very often result in fumbles by the passer. They can also have the psychological effect of causing hesitation and uncertainty and thereby affect the passer's rhythm.

Hands Up

When the passer raises the ball to throw it, the pass rusher should raise his hands and arms as high as he can. This action by the rusher can obstruct the passer's vision downfield or deflect the thrown ball. By raising the hands and arms the rusher can force the passer to throw the ball with a higher trajectory. This lofting of the ball means that the ball will not travel with the same velocity that it would when thrown unobstructed. A thrown ball that does not travel fast allows the pass defender more time to react and intercept the pass.

It is very important that the pass rusher keep his feet on the ground and not jump as he raises his hands. Since most quarterbacks are very athletic, they often pull the ball down and scramble when the rusher leaves his feet. Over the years I have seen many instances where a rusher breaks clean on the rush, raises his hands and jumps, and the passer pulls the ball down, ducks under the rusher and throws a touchdown pass.

If the passer is holding the ball as the pass rusher is approaching him, the rusher should drive his hands and arms down through the shoulder pads of the passer. Driving down through the shoulder pads prevents the passer from throwing the ball, and it also increases the chances he will fumble or lose control of the ball. The rusher should try to keep his face mask at the same level as that of the passer.

If the pass rusher concentrates on keeping his face mask at the same level as that of the passer, he will see the direction he is looking to throw. This will help him work into the throwing lane.

ADDITIONAL POINTS FOR THE PASS RUSHER

Draws and screens are reaction type of plays. Linemen do not defend the draw and screen, they react to them out of their pass-rush mode. Defensive ends should retrace their steps and try to square back up with the line of scrimmage and squeeze the running lane. Tackles or inside rushers should attempt to return to a two-gap mode, squared up with the line of scrimmage when they read draw.

The linemen must make the quarterback throw slow screens sooner than he wants to. On quick screens or hitch screens, linemen can be very effective with their hands up since the quarterback is throwing the ball relatively close to the line of scrimmage.

On all screens, as soon as the passer throws the ball the lineman should turn and go to the ball at the proper pursuit angle. Since the rushing linemen are not accounted for in the blocking schemes for screens, the rushers who recognize screens quickly and run to the ball can make tackles on these plays. Since the pass rushers usually make tackles from the side or from behind the ball carrier, very often these plays can result in fumbles.

The general role of inside pass rushers is to force the passer back in the pocket. Outside pass rushers have, as their major role, forcing the passer up, or toward the line of scrimmage. When quarterbacks use deep drops, the outside pass rushers, usually the ends, tend to have the greatest effect as pass rushers. This is due to the fact that the deep drop gives the outside speed rushers a better opportunity to use their speed to get to the passer. However, if the quarterback takes a three- or five-step drop, the inside rushers are more apt to have an effect on the passer than the outside rushers would. This is primarily due to the fact that the passer is throwing from a position so close to the line of scrimmage and is usually trying to throw over the raised hands and arms of the inside pass rushers.

Another important point for pass rushers to remember is that the quicker the pass blocker sets, the quicker the pass rusher should engage and make his move. If the blocker sets on the line of scrimmage, the rusher should engage the blocker and make his move quickly. On the other hand, if the pass blocker sets back, the rusher must sprint to the blocker and engage him before he makes his pass-rush move.

It is also important for the pass rusher to take a wider alignment whenever possible on sure-pass downs. This wider alignment puts greater pressure on the pass blocker and also forces him to compromise his parallel relationship with the line of scrimmage.

When the rusher breaks clean on the rush, he must not jump and be under control.

When the ball is thrown, all rushers must turn and run to the ball at the proper angle of pursuit.

From takeoff to the finish of the pass rush, the rusher should stay lower than the blocker—the rusher should always have the leverage advantage over his opponent if his shoulder level or face mask is lower. The rusher should not stretch his strength out by raising up.

Except for the power, or bull, rush, all pass-rush moves consist of some combination of push, pull or turn. Any combination is acceptable, but it is not sound to pull with both hands at the same time.

BASIC PASS-RUSH TECHNIQUES

Power, or Bull, Rush

On movement by the offense the rusher drives his hands forward, aiming for the outside upper tips of the front numbers on the blocker's jersey. The aiming point is the tips of the numbers to ensure that the arc of the hands is inside the hands and arms of the blocker. The objective is to get both hands inside those of the blocker.

The blow is struck with the palms and heels of the hands and must be delivered with enough power to force the offensive man backward, or at the minimum, shift his weight from the balls of his feet to his heels. This limits the blocker's ability to react quickly to changes of direction by the rusher. As the hands strike the blow, the elbows should lock, thereby bringing into use the additional force of the back muscles. It is important that the shoulder level of the rusher remain lower than that of the blocker at all times. This is accomplished by the pass rusher having good bend, or flexion, in the ankles, knees, and hips; a lower shoulder level ensures that the pass rusher will have more big-muscle involvement than the blocker and thereby ensure a leverage advantage. (See Photo 7-1.)

The rusher should use short, choppy steps while executing the power-rush technique. He should try to avoid long strides since they contribute to compromising the rusher's power base. All through the power rush, the rusher must have his weight distributed over his feet. This ensures that there will be maximum power and strength while executing the power-rush technique. The successful execution of the power-rush technique culminates with the pass rusher driving the blocker

PHOTO 7–1
Power, or bull, rush

into the passer before he can deliver the ball. As mentioned before, this power-rush technique is most effectively used by inside rushers versus the three- or five-step types of pass actions but can also be effective against deeper pass droppers. However, this technique can also be useful to outside rushers or defensive ends against defensive tackles who set soft or deep.

Turn and Rip or Turn and Swim

These pass-rush moves start as power or leverage rushes but develop into rushes over the corner of the blocker. These types of pass-rush techniques are used against pass protectors who are blocking for play-action as well as drop-back passes. Since the power rush against blockers and the two-gap technique versus run-blockers are essentially the same types of leverage techniques, they both lend themselves to evolving into these types of pass rushes. Most pass-rush moves that start as leverage rushes must ultimately involve speed or finesse over the corners, or edges, of the blockers to be successful.

All pass-rush moves over or through the blocker are some combination of push, pull and turn. By pushing with one hand and pulling with the other simultaneously, the rusher is accomplishing two things. One, he is turning the blocker and taking away the parallel relationship the blocker is trying to maintain with the line of scrimmage. When the pass protector can hold this position, he is forcing the rusher to take a long route around him to the passer. The other is that by turning the blocker he is exposing an edge, or corner, of the blocker to rush over.

If a rusher is going to make his move on the outside of the blocker off the power rush or two gap, he should pull with his outside hand and push with the inside. This push and pull turns the blocker and exposes the outside edge, or corner, of the blocker. As the pass blocker is being turned, the rusher takes a big step with his inside leg as close to the blocker as possible. It is important that the rusher burst, or accelerate, past the blocker as he turns him. By rubbing close to the blocker, the rusher is staying on a direct course to the passer as well as reducing the time the protector has to recover. [See Photos 7-2(a) and 7-2(b).]

There are two ways the pass rusher can use his inside hand or arm on an outside rush. One is the rip. With the rip-arm technique, the inside arm and shoulder are driven up through the outside arm and shoulder of the blocker. This action is similar to what is commonly known as an uppercut in boxing. The other is the swim, or arm-over, technique. With this type of action the inside arm is thrown over the outside shoulder of the blocker, much like the arm action used in freestyle swimming. It is important that the rip-arm or swim techniques be executed simultaneously with a pull with the other arm and a big step by the blocker. On inside rushes the pull is executed with the inside arm and the push and rip or swim with the outside arm. The shoulder level of the rusher must stay down throughout the rush. I think the rip-arm action should be taught first. With the

**PHOTO 7-2(a)
Pass rush: Turning
the blocker**

**PHOTO 7-2(b)
Pass rush: Turning
the blocker**

PHOTO 7-3
Pass rush: Rip technique

PHOTO 7-4
Pass rush: Swim technique

rip technique the rusher is more likely to keep his shoulder level down. Use of the swim technique usually causes rushers to raise up and thereby compromise their leverage advantage. Again, it is very important that the rusher using the swim move not raise up, keep his shoulder level down and not compromise his leverage advantage. (See Photos 7-3 and 7-4.)

The counter off the leverage or power rush involves engaging the blocker by striking a blow, faking either inside or outside, then rushing over the opposite corner of the blocker. With this move it is important that the rusher keep every aspect of the move upfield, or toward the blocker. There should be no flat or lateral movement by the rusher. In order for any rush technique to be effective, all aspects of the move must threaten the blocker with pressure. The blocker must always think there is a possibility that the rusher will attempt to power or run over him. This causes the blocker to firm up or set stronger, which reduces his ability to move his feet quickly and adjust to moves by the pass rusher. (See Photo 7-5.)

PHOTO 7-5
Pass rush: Countermove

Outside, or Gap, Rusher

Although inside pass rushers need to be able to combine the athletic qualities of speed and power, very often power becomes the dominant factor, whereas with outside, or gap, rushers speed, quickness and finesse dominate as qualities essential to effectiveness in this area. Strength and power certainly come into play but without speed, outside, or gap rushers, have very little chance to achieve at a high level.

Speed-Rush Techniques

It is important that the outside pass rusher line up with enough width to enable him, from a slightly pointed-in stance, to have a straight line to the passer. This angle or aiming point should be directly behind the center at the depth at which the quarterback sets to throw. Obviously, this aiming point changes with the opponent. If a team uses a lot of three- and five-step drops by the quarterback, the aiming point will be at a shallower angle, or closer to the line of scrimmage, than it would be if the opponent were a seven-step or deeper dropping team. It is very important that attention be paid to this factor in establishing a plan to rush the opponent's passer with the outside pass rushers.

Speed Rushing the Passer

As in all rush techniques, initial takeoff, or the ability to quickly gain ground on the offensive side of the line of scrimmage, is critical for outside, or gap, rushers. The rusher is literally trying to beat the offensive man out of his stance. The offensive blocker has to be made to fear that he will be beaten by the speed and quickness of the rusher around him on the outside.

Grab and Rub

The execution of this technique requires that the rusher reach to grab the outside arm and shoulder pad of the blocker

PHOTO 7-6
Grab-and-rub outside pass-rush technique

with his outside hand. As he grabs the blocker, the rusher should pull himself past him; simultaneously, he should lean into the blocker by dipping his inside shoulder. This dipping of the shoulder pressures the blocker and decreases the angle to the passer. The rusher should, as in all pass-rush techniques, take a big stride or step as he goes past the blocker. It is also important that the rusher stay low as he rubs or leans into the blocker. This ensures that he will have a leverage advantage and thereby decrease the angle or distance to the passer. (See Photo 7-6.)

Club Technique

In addition to grabbing with the outside hand, the speed rusher can club with his outside hand and turn the blocker. To execute this technique the rusher drives the outside hand and arm hard into the outside arm or shoulder pad of the blocker. This action is designed to turn the blocker and create a shorter, more direct lane to the passer.

Rip and Swim

In addition to the rub, or lean, technique, the rusher can use his inside arm to execute either a rip or a swim. The rip action with the inside arm is used to drive through the hands and arms of the pass blocker and help shorten the route to the passer. The swim action with the inside arm helps propel the rusher past the blocker. It, like the rip technique, also serves the purpose of removing the rusher's inside hand and arm from a position where the blocker could grab it.

Countermoves

The counter to the outside speed rush is the inside move on the blocker. Usually when a rusher establishes a hard upfield speed rush, the blocker tries to compensate by moving rapidly to the outside to block the rusher. This causes him to compromise his parallel relationship with the line of scrimmage and cross his feet over and prevents him from adjusting his feet to an inside move.

It is important that the rusher be patient and not hurry his move. He should aim to get to the tip of the outside shoulder of the blocker before he makes the inside move. After he forces the blocker to turn or cross his feet over, the rusher should either grab or club the inside shoulder or arm of the blocker with his inside hand and arm. Simultaneously, he should rub, rip or swim with his outside arm as he takes a big stride and moves past the blocker.

An additional point for pass rushers that is critical is that they must always be conscious of the pass blocker's hands and arms and be prepared to deal with them. Since the pass blocker is trying to use his hands and extended arms to control the pass rusher, it is often a good practice for the rusher to use his hands and arms to knock the blocker's hands off of him. This can be accomplished by driving his hands down, up or across the hands of the blocker during the pass-rush move.

All pass-rush moves that are effective come off of or utilize parts or all of, the elements described above. The techniques may vary somewhat, but the basic elements of takeoff (or initial quickness), elevation and pressure upfield, engaging the blocker or striking a blow, using the hands and feet, and accelerating in the move apply in virtually every circumstance.

Although some reference to pass rush off run blocks has been made in this chapter, most of this chapter has been devoted to pass rush against drop-back pass actions. In play-action, sprint-out, roll-out or bootleg passes, the same elements of technique apply. However, if aggressive blocking is being used, the various aspects of pass rush occur after the defender defeats the run blocker and recognizes pass.

8

Line-Charge Variations: Games and Stunts

Line-charge variations are subtle, but effective, ways to change the mode of operation for a defensive lineman. For example: A defensive tackle who aligns head up on an offensive guard is usually a two-gap player who has, as his primary responsibility, driving the guard back. After a few plays, the guard begins to anticipate this type of play from the defensive man and begins to employ various kinds of adjustments in his play to compensate or allow him to better block the defensive tackle. If, however, the tackle occasionally makes a quick inside move to the A gap or a quick outside move to the B gap on the snap of the ball, it makes the job of blocking him much more difficult for the offensive guard.

These types of variations can be used to accomplish two things. One, they can be used to cause the blocker to miss his block on the defender, thereby turning him loose to penetrate the gap and disrupt the offensive play. Two, they can be used to help the defensive player execute his primary technique (two gap) by causing the blocker to hesitate. The hesitation or uncertainty is caused by realization of the fact that just because the defender lines up in a two-gap mode does not necessarily mean he is going to employ that technique each time he lines up that way.

These line-charge variations can be executed by individual players or by the entire line as in slant defenses. In slant defensive schemes all the defensive linemen usually move either right or left to penetrate a gap on the snap of the ball.

When a lineman uses a slant charge, it will usually involve a linebacker compensating or changing gap responsibilities with the slanting lineman.

EXECUTION OF THE SLANT, OR GAP, TECHNIQUE

It is very important that the defensive lineman not give a signal of his intent to slant, or go to a gap charge, before the snap of the ball. The element of surprise is a strong asset in the successful execution of these types of change-up. There should be no deviation from the norm in terms of changes in stance, weight distribution, position of the hands and feet, or focus of the eyes.

To execute this technique the lineman should take a short six-inch parallel step in the direction he is going. This step should take place on movement by the offense, either the man or the ball. This step should be accompanied by a bigger step up the field toward the line of scrimmage with the opposite leg. Throughout the execution of this technique it is important that the shoulder level remain low, that the head and eyes be up and looking straight ahead and that the hips and shoulders be parallel with the line of scrimmage. Any other steps involved should be short six-inch steps as the defensive man reads the blocking scheme, defeats the blocker and goes to the ball.

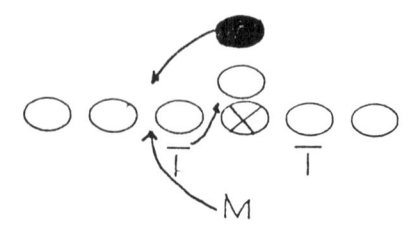

DIAGRAM 8-1

LINE-CHARGE VARIATIONS: GAMES AND STUNTS 91

In Diagram 8-1 the left defensive tackle is normally a two-gap player. That is, with runs designed to attack his side of the formation he is responsible for the B gap. However, he is executing an A gap charge, which means that at the snap of the ball he penetrates the A gap. The middle linebacker, whose normal responsibility is the A gap, now assumes the tackle's B gap responsibility on runs designed to attack his side of the formation.

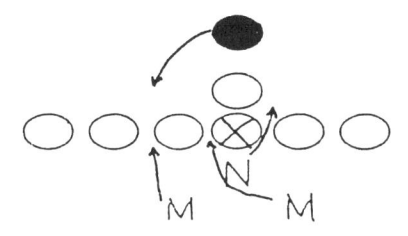

DIAGRAM 8-2

In Diagram 8-2 the nose tackle is normally a frontside or playside player. That is, he is responsible for the A gap to his left. However, he has been given a call that tells him to slant, or charge to the A gap to his right. The linebacker whose normal responsibility was the A gap to his side, or to the right, now assumes the responsibility for the A gap to the left of the center.

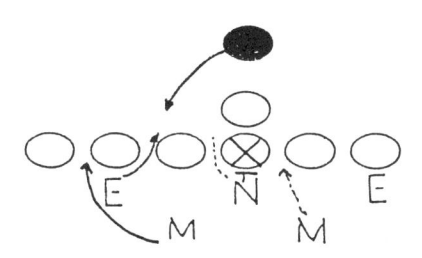

DIAGRAM 8-3

In Diagram 8-3 the left defensive end is normally responsible for the C gap on runs to his side of the formation. However, he has been given a B call, which tells him to slant to, or penetrate, the B gap on the snap of the ball. The linebacker whose normal responsibility is the B gap on runs to his side of the formation, now assumes the end's responsibility, the C gap.

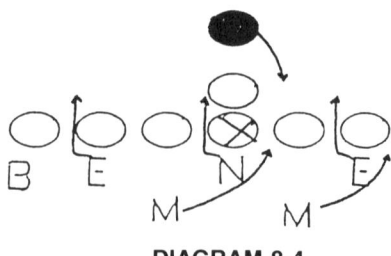

DIAGRAM 8-4

In Diagram 8-4 the defensive line is slanting to the tight-end side of the formation. The left end's gap responsibility does not change; he remains a C gap player. The nose tackle's gap responsibility changes since he is normally responsible for the A gap to the side of the play. He has an A call to his left, or away from the play. The right defensive end has a B call, or slant charge, to his left. His normal gap responsibility on runs to his side is the C gap. Therefore, his gap changes and becomes the responsibility of the right inside linebacker who is normally a B gap player on runs to his side. The left inside linebacker also has a change of gap responsibility on runs to the opposite side of the formation. When the nose tackle is in a normal two-gap mode, the left linebacker would be responsible for the left A gap. Since the nose tackle has been designated to slant to the left A gap, with this type of running play the left inside linebacker is responsible for the A gap on the right side of the formation.

Line-charge variations are designed to add variety to a defensive scheme. These variations are relatively simple ways to defend specific formations or offensive plays. A specific example of this would be giving a defensive left tackle an A call when the specific offensive formation indicates a strong possibility of a trap play to his side of the formation (Diagram 8-5).

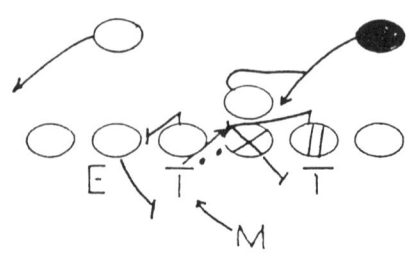

DIAGRAM 8-5

STUNTS: LINEMEN AND INSIDE LINEBACKERS

Stunts between defensive linemen and linebackers are other ways to either exchange gap responsibilities versus the run or to rush the passer. These are usually the most effective when they are executed between players who line up next to each other. For example, the most effective way to stunt the middle linebacker in a 4-3 defense would be to stunt him with one of the tackles (Diagram 8-6).

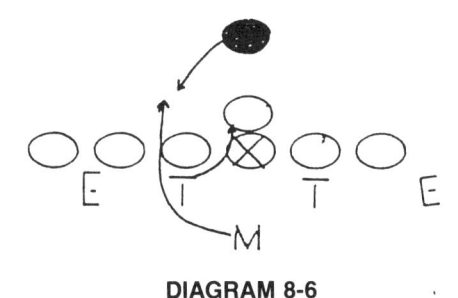

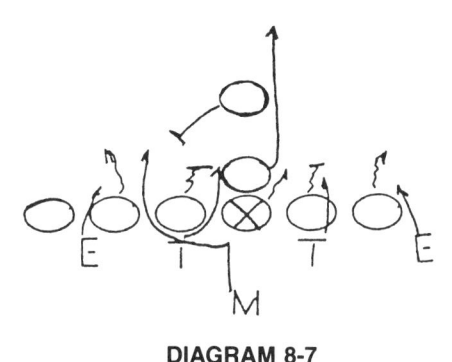

DIAGRAM 8-6

DIAGRAM 8-7

In Diagram 8-6 the middle linebacker is executing a stunt with the left defensive tackle. With a run to the tight-end side of the formation, or to the left, the tackle is normally a B gap player and the middle linebacker an A gap player. However, the executing of this stunt causes them to exchange their gap responsibilities on this type of running play. In run down situations the linebacker should go to his gap responsibility on the snap of the ball. On sure-pass downs these stunts are more effective if the lineman goes fast, or at the snap, and the linebacker starts straight ahead or as in Diagram 8-7, heads straight at the center a step or two and then makes a tight move to the B gap. By threatening the line of scrimmage with his initial action, the linebacker has a tendency to freeze the center by making him think the linebacker is going to rush straight over him. This action also allows time for a short corner to develop since, as the defensive tackle makes an inside move, the guard will have a tendency to collapse or block down on the tackle. This creates a shorter course or straighter line or lane to the passer. As the linebacker rushes the passer, it is very important that he keep all of his movement downhill or toward the line of scrimmage throughout the execution of these stunts. It is also important that he not give the stunt away or tip his intent to the offense. He must line up to execute any of these types of stunts just as he would when he is not stunting.

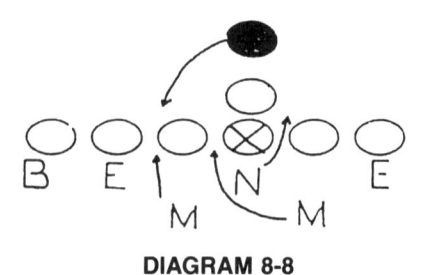

DIAGRAM 8-8

In Diagram 8-8 the right-side, inside linebacker and the nose tackle are executing a stunt that was either called in the huddle or audibilized on the line of scrimmage. The nose tackle is stunting to his right, or to the weakside A gap, and the right-side, inside linebacker is stunting or blitzing into the left-side A gap on the snap of the ball. Since the nose tackle is normally a frontside or playside A gap player, this particular stunt changes the nose tackle's and right linebacker's gap responsibilities on a run designed to attack the defensive left. In Diagram 8-9 a stunt is executed between the nose tackle who is moving to the left A gap and the left linebacker who is stunting into the right A gap.

LINE-CHARGE VARIATIONS: GAMES AND STUNTS 95

DIAGRAM 8-9

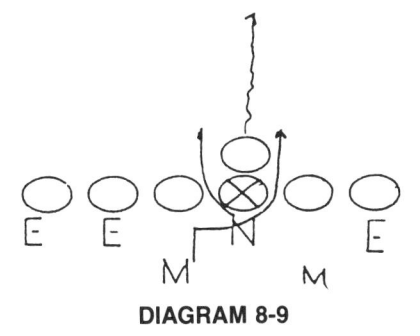

Since this stunt is shown executed against a pass play, the left inside linebacker will move toward the guard and try to threaten him, thereby allowing time for the action of the nose to shorten his angle to the passer.

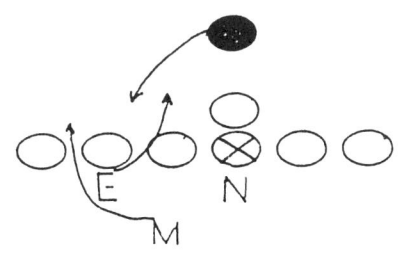

DIAGRAM 8-10

In Diagram 8-10 the defensive end slants, or charges, into the B gap on the snap of the ball. His normal gap responsibility on running plays to his side is the C gap. On plays designed to attack the opposite side his responsibility is the B gap. With this type of stunt he is responsible for the B gap on both types of running plays. The left inside linebacker's normal gap responsibility on plays designed to attack his side is the B gap, but with this stunt he is responsible for the C gap on plays to his side of the formation.

In Diagram 8-11 this same stunt is executed in a sure-pass situation. The action of the end is the same as it is versus the run. The linebacker, however, will threaten the guard straight ahead before he attacks the C gap as a pass rusher. The defensive end becomes an inside pass rusher with this stunt, and the linebacker becomes an outside or contain pass rusher.

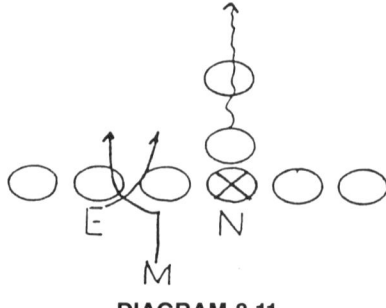

DIAGRAM 8-11

STUNTS: LINEMEN AND OUTSIDE LINEBACKERS

Linemen can also be involved in running stunts with linebackers who line up on the line of scrimmage. An example of this type of stunt would be one between the outside linebacker and the defensive end in a 4-3 defense or 3-4 defense (Diagrams 8-12 and 8-13).

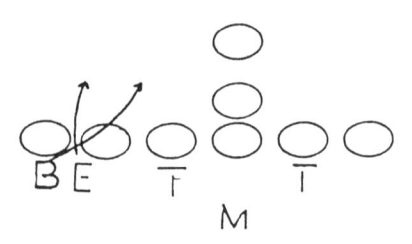

DIAGRAM 8-12

DIAGRAM 8-13

In Diagrams 8-12 and 8-13, on the snap of the ball, the defensive end charges hard up the field, becomes a C gap player and is either the force man or the cutback man on running plays depending on the pass coverage. On passing plays he is the outside or contain rusher. The defensive end is first and the linebacker is the second man in this stunt. On the snap of the ball the outside linebacker takes a short jab step with his inside foot to ensure that the tight end does not cut him off. He should then take a short step with his outside leg to square up. Next from his position with his hips and shoulders parallel with the line of scrimmage, he should accelerate through the C gap to the ball. On pass plays he is an inside pass rusher on his side of the formation.

These are just a few examples of how the line charges of defensive lineman can be varied. These simple changes in line charges are effective ways to place defensive linemen in positions to make plays. These change-up calls are usually made to take advantage of blocking schemes, formation tendencies or personnel matchups.

Stunts are used as change-ups as well. They are usually more effective if they are used infrequently and are accompanied by the element of surprise. Again, they are used to give the defense some type of advantage in stopping the opponent's running plays or rushing their passer.

GAMES BETWEEN DEFENSIVE LINEMEN

Games involve the exchanging of gap responsibilities between linemen versus running plays and the exchanging of pass-rush lane responsibilities against passing plays. These games can be effective against the run as well as the pass.

There are some general rules that apply to running games effectively. One is that the linemen who are executing the games should not tip off their intent. Games are always more effective if they catch the offensive team by surprise. Also, if a game is being executed in a run down situation, it should be a quick game. That is, there should be very little delay by the second man in the game. In addition, all the movement should be toward the line of scrimmage as the linemen execute their game. It is also important that they not raise up or compromise their leverage position from the start to the finish of the game.

When games are used in pass-rush situations, there are a few additional points that are important. One is that the shorter the drop by the quarterback, the quicker the game must be run. Since the three- or five-step passing teams usually are short, or quick, setters, the most effective types of games against them are quick games designed to get in the face of the quarterback with the inside rushers quickly. The general rule is that the shorter the set by the offensive pass blocker, the quicker the game. By the same token, if a team is a seven-step-drop team, the line will be soft setters; with soft setters or deep-pass-setting linemen it is desirable to sprint to the blocker, then execute the game. Against this type of pass protection, delayed types of games can be effective. These types of delay games consist of both players starting to attack their blockers and then executing the game after they have crossed the line of scrimmage.

On pass-rush games it is important to know how the offense picks up games. If they pick up games using a man-for-man scheme, the man who goes first should drive at an angle to pick or cut off the blocker assigned to block the second man in the game. If the opponent is zone-blocking games, then the man who goes first should try to grab or pull the man he is lined up over as he works upfield. That is, he should try to remove the man he is lined up over from the position he wants to occupy to pick up the second man in the game. The general rules here are that with man blocking get as far away as possible from the blocker while working to pick or cut off the man assigned to block the second man in the game. With zone blocking, the first man in the game should stay as close as possible to the man he lines up over as he executes the game. He will try to pull the blocker by grabbing him and throwing him out of the area he is protecting.

Tackle—Tackle Games

Games between the defensive tackles in an even defense, like a 4-3, can be effective when executed against inside running plays like quick-hitting dive or trap plays. These games are most effective against trap plays when the tackle who goes first is the one who is going to be trapped. For example: On a trap that is designed to have the left offensive guard trapping the left defensive tackle, he is the one who should be going first in a game. Where the trap is coming from or which guard is doing the trapping is usually predictable by the offensive formation, therefore it is possible to be accurate in designating which tackle goes first in a game. The effect of sending first the tackle who is meeting the trapper is that the velocity and momentum he generates will cause him to meet the guard and close the trap hole. Against base blocking, or man-for-man blocking or dive-blocking schemes, it makes very little difference which tackle goes first.

Games between the tackles run versus the pass can be called for a variety of reasons. The most obvious one is to create pressure or rush the quarterback. Versus even defenses, the center is many times freed up to assist the guards in blocking the defensive tackles. The tackle–tackle game is a way to try to nullify the advantage the offense has by having the extra blocker available. The game also gives the defense a better chance for success when one or both of the guards are dominant players. The tackle–tackle game is often a good tool to tie up or involve the center and both guards when the defensive team is dogging or blitzing. The center is usually designated to block a blitzing linebacker or secondary player in most drop-back blitz pickups versus even defenses. By running a tackle–tackle game the defense can usually cause the center to stay to help block the game thereby turning loose the linebacker or secondary player he is responsible for.

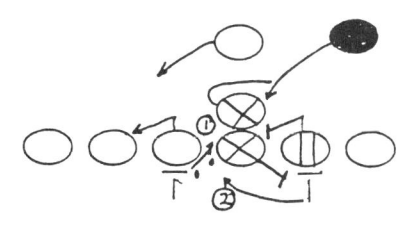

DIAGRAM 8-14

Diagram 8-14 illustrates a trap play. In this diagram the left guard is the trap blocker, and the left defensive tackle is the man going first in the game.

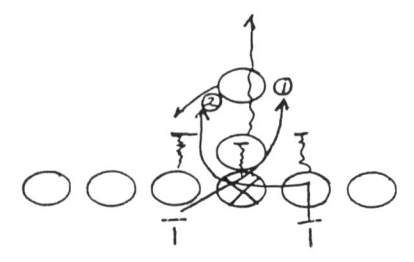

DIAGRAM 8-15

Diagram 8-15 is a tackle–tackle game run against drop-back pass protection. The aiming point for the tackle who goes first should be to charge through the near shoulder of the offensive center. His first step should be a short, jab step with his inside leg. He needs to have enough power, velocity and leverage to squeeze or collapse the center back into the far A gap if he elects to block back on him. His second step should be a short step with his outside foot to square up. He should then continue upfield and become the inside rusher to the opposite side of the formation. The right tackle should take a jab step with his inside leg toward the line of scrimmage allowing time for the left tackle's charge to shorten his route to the passer. After taking a short step with his outside leg to square up with the line of scrimmage, he should accelerate to become the inside rusher on the opposite side of the formation.

The tackle–tackle game is designed to give the tackles an opportunity to exchange rush lanes and to give them a tool to confuse and defeat blockers. These games must be executed with good leverage and speed. It is important that the tackles remember they are merely exchanging rush lanes and that they need to be conscious of balance in this regard at all times. These types of games are effective versus all types of passing schemes but are most effective against the short-drop teams whose quarterback is operating close to the line of scrimmage. They are designed to give quick pressure in front of the passer.

End–Tackle Games

Games between the tackles and ends are effective in both run and pass situations. The 3-4 defense and the 4-3 defenses

LINE-CHARGE VARIATIONS: GAMES AND STUNTS 101

lend themselves to these games. One of the problems with running games between the defensive end and nose tackle in a 3-4 defense is the fact that the distance between the end and the nose is so great. In the 3-4 defense the nose tackle's normal alignment is head up on the center and the defensive end lines up in a 5 or 6 alignment on the offensive tackle. The fact that they are so far apart in their alignment can cause problems in executing games. When executing a tackle–end game where the nose tackle goes first, there is always a danger the uncovered guard will pin the nose tackle or prevent him from completing his part of the game and assuming the defensive end's run-gap or pass-rush lane responsibilities. In the 3-4 defense the end going first is by far the best game between the end and nose tackle. It is not advisable to run the game with the nose going first. The reason the nose-first game is not desirable is that, as mentioned before, there is always the danger that the guard will pin the nose and prevent him from working through the B gap.

3-4 defense games

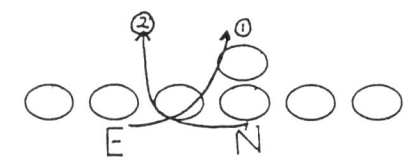

DIAGRAM 8-16

In Diagram 8-16 the defensive end and nose tackle in a 3-4 defense are executing a game. The end goes first in this game, and the nose is second. On the snap of the ball the end should take a step toward the offensive guard and drive through the guard's outside shoulder. His hips and shoulders should be parallel with the line of scrimmage as he executes this game. The nose tackle should take a short jab step toward the center and at the same time flash his hands at the center to make him think that he is rushing over him. This flashing of the center has the effect of freezing or holding the center as well as allowing time for the lane to the passer to collapse or shorten. As the end drives through the B gap, the offensive tackle will close or move to the inside as he blocks him. This is how the route to the passer will be shortened for the nose tackle. As the nose works toward the B gap, he should keep his shoulder level down, his hips and shoulders parallel with the line of scrimmage, and there should be very little movement laterally. As with all techniques executed by defensive linemen, movement of defensive players must be toward the offense. The intent is to play as much of the game as possible on the offensive side of the line of scrimmage. The nose will assume the pass-rush lane responsibilities of the defensive end. Versus the run, the end should be in a position to defeat any blocker who is trying to block him from the inside, such as the near guard or the far guard on a trap play. If the offensive tackle tries to block down on him on running plays, he should plant his inside leg, flatten his route and pursue the ball carrier. This should all happen behind the offensive line of scrimmage.

4-3 defense games between ends and tackles

In the 4-3 defense the defensive tackle and end line up on adjacent offensive linemen. The proximity of these players to each other enables them to game effectively. Because they line up next to each other, they are able to run a variety of types of games. They can run games fast or delay parts of them. In addition, the games can be equally effective regardless of which player goes first—the end or tackle.

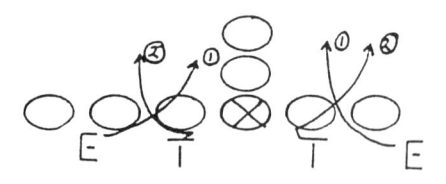

DIAGRAM 8-17

Diagram 8-17 is an end–tackle game with the end going first and the tackle second. This the most frequently used game in the 4-3 defense. The aiming point for the end is the near shoulder of the offensive guard. On movement by the offense the defensive end steps with his inside leg at about a forty-five degree angle toward the near shoulder of the offensive guard. The second step should be a short step with the outside leg to square up. He should drive through the B gap and work to squeeze any block out by the near guard, block back by the center or trap block from the far guard. He should meet these types of blocks with his inside forearm and shoulder pad. I do not believe the end should use the outside arm to close these types of blocks. As I said earlier, taking these types of blocks on with the outside arm causes the defender to compromise his squared-up position with the line of scrimmage, giving himself up and therefore eliminating any chance to shed the blocker and make a tackle. On running plays, if the tackle blocks down on the end as he moves inside, he should penetrate, plant his inside foot and flatten his course to the ball carrier. On pass plays the end is the inside rusher to his side of the formation. He assumes the tackle's pass-rush responsibilities.

The defensive tackle should take a jab step toward the offensive guard and at the same time flash him with his hands. Again, these actions by the tackle should cause some hesitation by the guard and at the same time allow the corner to shorten or collapse so that he has a more direct route to the passer. As the tackle turns up the field, his hips and shoulders should be parallel with the line of scrimmage. On running plays outside to his side of the formation, he should penetrate and pursue at the best angle he can take to get to the ball carrier. On running plays to the opposite side of the formation, he should plant his outside foot and flatten his route to the ball carrier.

On pass plays the tackle is the outside or contain rusher to his side of the formation.

DIAGRAM 8-18

Diagram 8-18 is an end–tackle game that is being run versus a team that uses deep drops by the quarterback and soft sets by the pass protectors. With this type of pass action, delayed types of games are at times effective. These types of games are executed by both linemen, the end and tackle, driving straight ahead toward the offensive guard and tackle. The end should flash his hands at the offensive tackle as he steps at him. As soon as the tackle sets to take a stand, the defensive end should drive hard through the B gap and execute the game. The defensive tackle should try to engage the offensive guard with his hands and read the defensive end. As soon as the defensive end clears through the B gap, the defensive tackle accelerates off the guard, rubs tight to the offensive tackle and rushes the passer as the outside or contain rusher to his side of the formation.

Any pass-rush games can be run quick or delayed. Quick games can be effective versus any type of running play or pass action. Delayed games are most effective against teams whose passer takes deep drops. It is a waste of time to run delayed games against three- and five-step-drop teams since the quarterback is getting rid of the ball so fast. Usually, if a delayed game is being executed and the opponent runs the ball, the defensive linemen do not go through with the game. They will read the running play and then play their normal run-gap responsibilities.

Games with the ends going first and the tackles second are usually most effective when the offensive tackle is a relatively deep pass protector, and the offensive guard is a shallow or firm setter on or near the line of scrimmage. The natural separation between the tackle and guard in the pass set creates the opportunity for the defensive end to penetrate and drive through the guard with his initial charge. This has the effect of flattening the corner or shortening the route the tackle has to the passer.

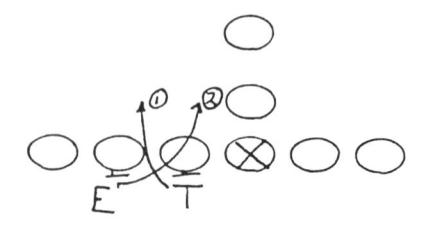

DIAGRAM 8-19

LINE-CHARGE VARIATIONS: GAMES AND STUNTS 105

Diagram 8-19 is an example of a tackle–end game with the defensive tackle going first. Also, though the end–tackle games are used more frequently, the tackle–end games are very effective in some situations. Specifically, when the guard and the tackle are both firm pass setters, these games are the most effective. When the pass blocking is done in this manner, the tackle can penetrate the B gap, shield the offensive tackle and allow the defensive end to penetrate as an inside pass rusher. If the offensive tackle is a soft setter, he is able to read the game quickly, slide inside and block the defensive end or tackle.

The aiming point for the defensive tackle is the near shoulder of the offensive tackle. His first step should be with his outside leg at about forty-five degrees toward the near shoulder of the offensive tackle. He then employs all the factors that apply to the first man in a game. He will become the outside or contain rusher to his side of the formation. The end will take a step toward the offensive tackle; he should flash his hands and execute his portion of the game, which will result in his rushing the passer as an inside rusher to his side of the formation.

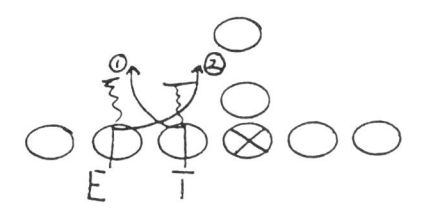

DIAGRAM 8-20

This game can also be run as a delayed game (Diagram 8-20). As in all delayed games, both the end and the tackle drive their hands and sprint to the blocker they are lined up over. The tackle then will drive hard through the B gap. The end may actually engage the offensive tackle. He must avoid being held by the tackle. As the defensive end engages the offensive tackle, he must read the defensive tackle. As the tackle makes his move into the B gap, the defensive end should shed the tackle and accelerate through the inside rush lane on his side of the formation.

It is very important that the defensive tackle squeeze the C gap on any down block or penetrate and flatten his route to the ball carrier on any perimeter run to his side of the formation.

THREE-MAN GAMES

Games that involve three adjacent linemen can be effective against pass offenses that utilize deep drops by the quarterback. These games, like two-man games, involve the exchanging of run-gap and pass-rush responsibilities between the players who are executing them. These types of games fall into two general categories. One is the type of game where two defensive linemen slant or rush through gaps toward another lineman who is responsible to assume the run-gap and pass-rush lane responsibility of the man farthest from him in the game. An example of this would be the left end and left tackle making inside rush moves to their right, and the right defensive tackle becoming the outside rusher on the left side of the formation (Diagram 8-21). Another example of this type of game would be both tackles making rush moves to their left and the left end having the responsibility to become the inside pass rusher on the right side of the formation (Diagram 8-22).

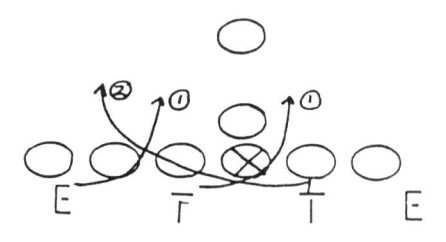

DIAGRAM 8-21

Responsibilities
Right Tackle—outside rusher, left side
Left Tackle—inside rusher, right side
Left End—inside rusher, left side

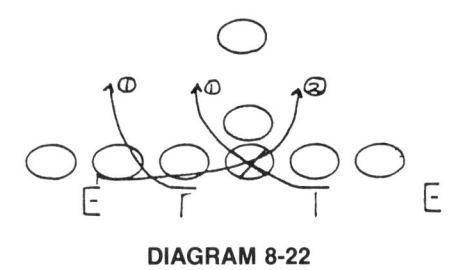

DIAGRAM 8-22

Responsibilities
Right Tackle—inside rusher, left side
Left Tackle—outside rusher, left side
Left End—inside rusher, right side

In Diagram 8-21 the left tackle and the left end go on the snap of the ball. It is important that the right tackle be patient, flash the guard and let the corner he will be rushing over shorten or collapse. He has a long way to go to become the outside rusher to his left. The more patient he is, the more his route will be shortened.

In Diagram 8-22 the right tackle and the left tackle will make their move to the left on the snap of the ball. The left end will flash the offensive tackle, allow the corner to shorten and become the inside rusher on the right side of the formation.

Three-man games were most useful tools to pressure the quarterback when there was a preponderance of deep-dropping pass-offense schemes. The quick passing games and three- and five-step drops by the quarterback have caused defenses to all but abandon the use of three-man games.

SUMMARY

In this chapter I have covered the principles involved in executing line-charge variations, stunts and games. I have also included examples of these various kinds of change-ups. There are obviously combinations of variations, stunts and games that can be used in addition to those mentioned in this chapter.

Every defensive scheme lends itself to these types of variations or change-ups. The critical factors that contribute to success in execution in these areas are:

1. Pre-snap read—don't tip off your intent before the snap.
2. Execute all phases of the charges toward the line of scrimmage.
3. Play as much of the game as possible with the hips and shoulders parallel with the line of scrimmage.
4. The first man in a game or stunt should get as much penetration as possible quickly.
5. The second man in a game or stunt must be patient and allow time to have his routes collapsed or shortened.
6. It is desirable to have the element of surprise as much as possible. Line-charge variations, stunts and games should be used as change-ups to a base scheme.

9

Defensive Line Drills

I believe the beginning of every practice should be devoted to providing opportunities for players to prepare their bodies for the rigors of practice. There is no question in my mind that this is time well spent. There are two critical reasons for these activities. One is that a player who is stretched and warmed up is better prepared to execute at a high level. The other is that players who are properly prepared physically for practice are less likely to be injured.

WARM-UP

Individual coaches should put their players through a short series of movement exercises to warm them up. The defensive line coach should put his players through a series of warm-up running exercises that consist of a high-knee action jog, a carioca on the line, crossovers to increase the flexion in the hips, a quick-feet hip-turn drill and a backpedal-turn drill. These drills are all conducted on a line like a yard line or sideline, and each phase should cover a distance of about ten yards. Players do each drill up and back or for ten yards in one direction and then return to the starting point repeating the drill. These drills are designed to stretch and loosen the big muscles below the waist. This is the area that big men must continually work to keep loose because of the development in this area as a result of weight training. This period should not exceed five minutes (Diagram 9-1).

Defensive Line: Line Drills

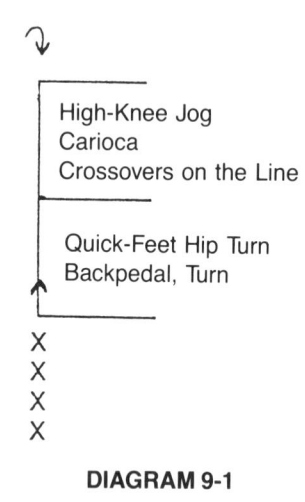

```
              ↑
         ┌─────────────────────
         │  High-Knee Jog
         │  Carioca
         │  Crossovers on the Line
         ├─────────────────────
         │  Quick-Feet Hip Turn
         │  Backpedal, Turn
       ↑ │
         └─────────────────────
        X
        X
        X
        X
```

DIAGRAM 9-1

Stretching

Stretching exercises are designed to loosen and stretch the parts of the body the players will be using in practice. These exercises are essential in that specific muscle groups are isolated and prepared for the stress that will be placed on them in practice. This period need not be any longer than ten minutes.

MOVEMENT DRILLS

The ability to move quickly is an essential quality all good defensive players possess. Associated with the ability to move quickly is the ability to change directions quickly. Since defense is, to a large degree, reaction or response to the actions of the offense, the quicker a defender reacts the more effective he will be in making plays to stop the offense.

One of the most critical factors in changing directions quickly is the ability of the defensive player to play the game with his body weight distributed over the balls of his feet. Good flexion at the ankles, knees and hips enables him to achieve this desirable body balance.

Although quickness and speed are, to a degree, God-given physical attributes, there is no doubt in my mind that they can be improved. As a player becomes increasingly aware of the role that body position and weight distribution play in these areas, and the more he works and drills to improve them, the more he will continue to improve and it will be reflected in his productivity on the football field.

Wave Drill

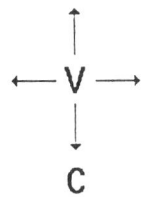

```
        ↑
        |
   ← — V — →
        |
        ↓
        C
```

DIAGRAM 9-2

From the up position with good flexion at the ankles, knees and hips, the player begins the drill by working his feet rapidly on a command by the coach. The coach then gives him signals with a ball or with his hands to move right, left, backward or forward. The player's feet should move rapidly throughout the drill. He should always move the lead leg and never cross his feet over. When he changes directions side-to-side, he should always plant and drive off his outside leg. This drill should be conducted on a line on the field. There should always be square or sharp changes of direction. It is important that the player not raise his shoulder level as he executes this drill.

The Wave Drill can begin with the player working his feet, then dropping to the ground on his stomach, on a command by the coach, then getting up and working his feet and proceeding through all the movements described above. Adding the dropping to the ground to the drill is designed to emphasize to the player that defensive players will be on the ground at times for various reasons due to the physical-contact nature of the game. All players, at one time or another, are on the ground. This drill teaches players to get up rapidly and proceed to move in a hitting position. (See Diagram 9-2.)

Although defensive linemen spend most of their time executing their responsibilities with their hand on the ground, it is important that they learn how to move as a football player in the up, two-point or hitting position.

Takeoff Drills

Takeoff drills are not very complicated but I cannot think of a more important area to work on with defensive linemen. Takeoff drills are designed to improve the initial reaction of defensive players. It is very important that the coach place the players in an environment in practice that is as close as possible to real game situations. This is best accomplished by the coach or manager snapping a ball and at the same time using a variety of cadences to simulate the quarterback's action at the snap. Although the cadence has no significance, as far as takeoff is concerned, it does get the defensive lineman accustomed to hearing a snap count as he concentrates on the ball for movement.

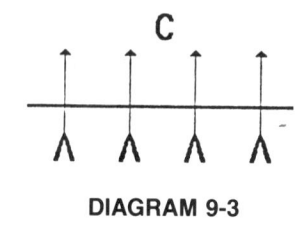

DIAGRAM 9-3

DIAGRAM 9-4

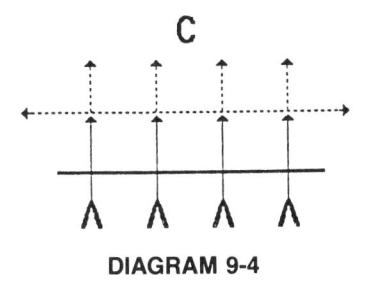

On movement, the lineman should explode across the line of scrimmage (Diagram 9-3). He should keep his shoulder level down. The objective is to gain as much ground as possible on the first two steps. He should push off his back foot and roll over his front foot. By rolling over his front foot, I mean he should get a surge or push off the front foot as well as the back. This equalizing of the pressure on both feet during takeoff prevents slipping that occurs when the player only pushes off the back foot. On this drill the player should sprint through five yards and finish the drill at about ten yards.

Takeoff drills can be combined with a wave drill. This drill requires that two people be involved in directing it—one to snap the ball and give the cadence, the other to give hand signals or use a ball for reaction. In this drill (Diagram 9-4) the defensive linemen take off, sprint for five yards, come under control and then execute all of the elements of the wave drill as they are illustrated in Diagram 9-2.

Again, it is very important that these drills be performed on lines similar to those on a football field with lines every five yards. These lines serve as a good way for the coach and players to judge the relative speed, quickness and movement ability of the players. Takeoff, or initial quickness, drills should be done every practice every day. They are important because this is where it all starts for defensive linemen. The defensive lineman is striving to attack the offensive team and play as much of the game as possible on the offensive side of the line of scrimmage. The offensive players know when the ball will be snapped because they know the snap count. The defensive player can nullify this advantage by great takeoff, or initial quickness. With concentration and repetition every player's initial quickness can be improved.

Bag Drills

Movement drills over obstacles like small cylinders or other types of dummies are valuable in the training and conditioning of defensive linemen for several reasons. One is that defensive linemen spend a lot of time working with heavy weights and therefore have well-developed lower bodies. In my opinion, these big-muscle groups need to be worked and flexibility increased in these areas. Movement drills, over obstacles, are a very good way to accomplish this. Another reason to run these drills is that the area in which defensive linemen usually operate is like an obstacle course. These drills assist defensive players in developing the ability to step over obstacles without having to look down at them. In other words, they develop an extra sense or feel for moving in an area that is filled with obstructions.

High Step Over Bags

In Diagram 9-5 four dummies are placed about one and one-half yards apart in a straight line. The defensive linemen line up at one end of the dummies. They sprint over the dummies exaggerating picking up their knees, taking as many rapid steps between the dummies as they can, and finish by sprinting five yards hard over the last dummy. After all players have completed the course, the line turns around and repeats the drill in the other direction. This drill tends to contribute to loosening up the lower body or big muscles of the linemen. (See Photo 9-1.)

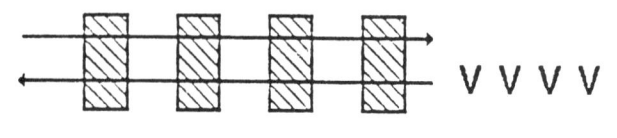

DIAGRAM 9-5

DEFENSIVE LINE DRILLS 115

PHOTO 9-1
High step over bags

Quick Feet Over Dummies

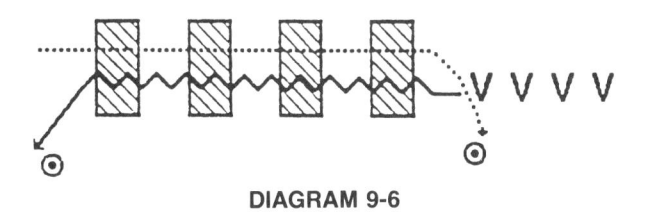

DIAGRAM 9-6

In Diagram 9-6 the same four dummies are used. However, cones are added in front of the dummies five yards from the front of the dummies on each end. The object of this drill is for the players to move their feet as rapidly as they can in the space between the dummies. The players begin in a good hitting position working their feet rapidly. On command they begin working over the dummies and continuing to move their feet as rapidly as they can, taking as many short, choppy steps as possible between the dummies. They should develop a rapid rhythm and always pick their lead leg up, not cross over, as they move through the dummies. They should keep their shoulder level down all the way through the drill with good flexion at the ankles, knees and hips. It is very important that they finish the drill correctly. The object of this drill is to increase flexibility in the big muscles as well as develop the ability to move over the obstacle course, that is, the line of scrimmage, without having to look down at the dummies. In addition, after they have cleared the last dummy, the players should accelerate and sprint past the cone toward the line of scrimmage. The players must understand they are working over these obstacles to ultimately get to the ball carrier. By sprinting over the last dummy, and for five yards after that, the player is made aware that one of the purposes of this drill is to emphasize pursuit and working up the field after clearing the obstacles that are present along the line of scrimmage.

Another important point worth discussing here is the acquisition of discipline in executing drills. One of the most critical areas where defensive football players fail is in finishing plays. If coaches establish a specific finish they will demand on each drill, they will go a long way toward preparing their players to finish plays when they are actually playing the game.

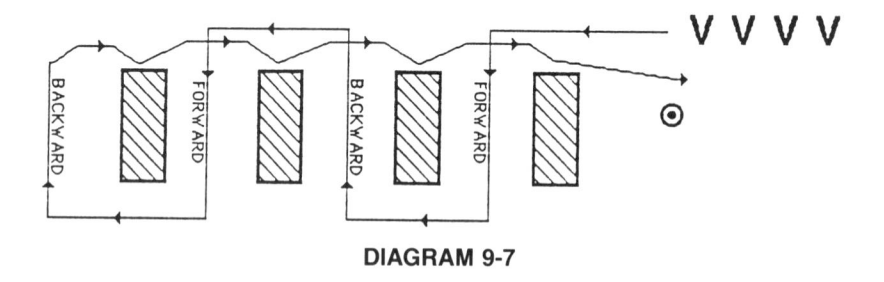

DIAGRAM 9-7

The same four dummies are used for the drill illustrated in Diagram 9-7. This drill is also a movement drill from the up position. The defensive player sprints forward to the front of the area between the first two dummies. He backpedals through the lane between the dummies. He then sprints through the next lane and backpedals through the last one. He then shuffles down the line striking the top portion of each dummy. His feet should be constantly moving as he works down the line. He finishes the drill by sprinting five, hard yards beyond the cone placed out from the end of the dummies. It is important that he keep his shoulder level down through the sprint and backpedal phases of the drill. It is also important that he have good flexion at the ankles, knees and hips as he touches the dummies and on the five-yard sprint past the cone.

Individual Waves Over the Dummies

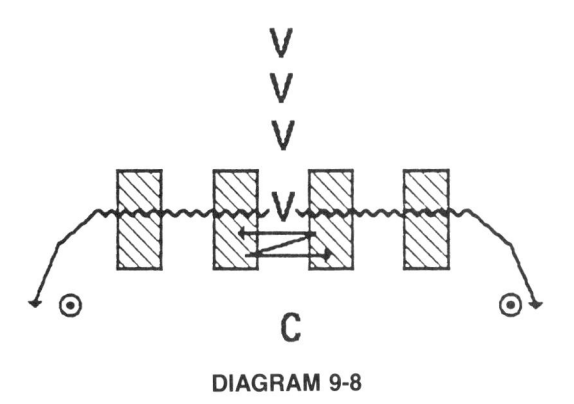

DIAGRAM 9-8

The four dummies with the cones off the front corners five yards away is the equipment used for the drill illustrated in Diagram 9-8. The players execute this drill, individually reacting to the hand signals of the coach or to a ball he uses to indicate the type of direction changes desired. The player starts in the middle lane working his feet rapidly in a good hitting position. The coach gives him a signal indicating the direction he wants the player to move. The player reacts by moving into the next area between dummies, working his feet. A move by the coach signals the player to move over one dummy. It is important that the player always move by picking up his near leg and not by crossing his feet over. It is also important that the player continually move his feet in a rapid fashion. After the player has

PHOTO 9–2
Quick-feet, individual-over-the-dummies drill

moved over three or four dummies, the coach should extend his arm to the right or left. The player should respond by working his feet over the dummies in that direction. When he crosses the last dummy, he should accelerate and sprint past the cone, keeping his hips and shoulders as parallel as he can with the line of scrimmage. This drill can also be concluded with the coach signaling the player to backpedal and then rush the passer. The coach simulates a passing action, and the player responds by raising his hands and arms. When the drill is finished in this fashion, it is important that the pass rusher raise his hands without leaving his feet. This, again, helps the player develop the discipline essential to getting his hands up and not jumping when the passer raises the ball. (See Photo 9-2.)

SLED DRILLS

It is absolutely essential that some type of sled with flat pads be available to teach techniques to defensive linemen. The best sleds available are those that have some type of relatively big, flat pad with jersey numbers on them. These sleds are available with anywhere from a single pad to seven pads on them. The obvious value of multipad sleds is that more players can work at the same time. The simulated jersey numbers are valuable in that they are aiming points for hand placement as the player strikes with his hands.

Teaching the Hands

Knees

The hands technique is described in detail in Chapter 3. The first phase of this technique involves the player assuming a position on the knees in front of a pad on the sled. His back should be relatively straight and the player's arms and hands should hang loose in front of him. He should place his hands at the outside tips of the numbers to get a fit or feel. After he gets a feel for the fit, he executes the technique, striking on the movement of a ball by the coach. He should always lock out after he strikes with his hands. After locking out the arms, he should roll his hips into the blow, thereby involving the big muscles of the lower body. It is important that all movement of the hands and arms be forward and that there be no hitching or winding up. It is also important that the head and eyes of the player remain at the same level throughout the execution of the technique and that the player hold his position with his hands on the sled for five or ten seconds after he strikes the blow. He will feel the power he can generate if he does this. If he merely slaps the pad with his hands, he will not experience the feeling of power that the technique can generate. (See Photos 9-3, 9-4, and 9-5.)

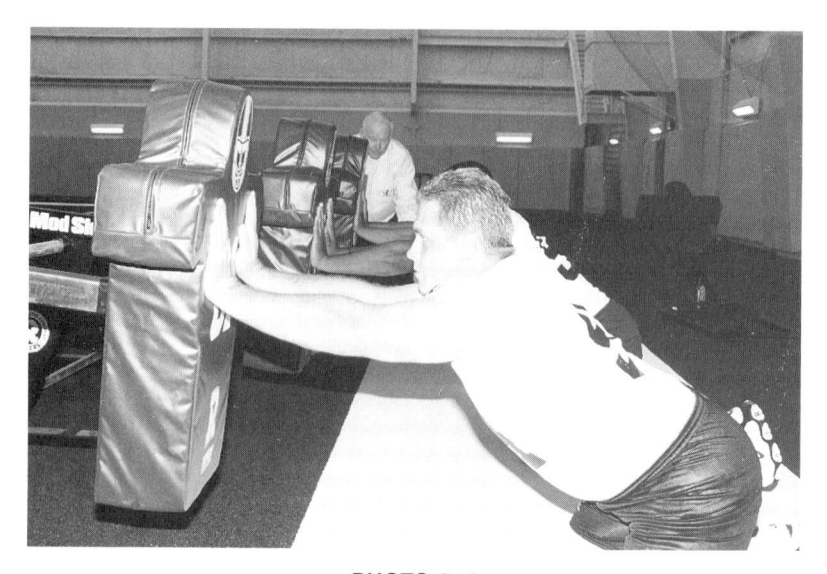

PHOTO 9-3
Hands technique, knees: The fit on sled

PHOTO 9-4
Hands technique, knees: Strike and lock out

PHOTO 9-5
Hands technique, knees: Strike, lock out and roll hips

Up position—no feet

The next phase of teaching the hands is for the player to assume a stance in front of a pad on the sled. From this position he places his hands at the outside tips of the numbers on the pad to get a fit. Just as he did from the knees, he should extend his arms, lock out at the elbows and roll his hips in to feel the power of the technique. Next the coach should give him movement and he should strike a blow with the hands, lock out at the elbows and roll his hips in as he holds his hands at the tips of the numbers. As he did from the knees, he should keep his head and eyes in the same relative position throughout the execution of the technique.

Up position—bring the feet

The next phase of teaching the hands on a sled involves all the segments described above with the addition of the player finishing the drill by taking the proper steps. I like to describe this process as the player attacking with his hands and then bringing his feet with him. These steps should be a series of six-inch steps with the player finishing with his inside leg forward and a short stagger or toe-and-heel relationship with the other foot. It is important to emphasize that the player should keep his shoulder and head and eye levels constant throughout the drill.

Up position—bring the feet—pursuit

The final drill in this series of hand sled drills involves pursuit at the end of the drill. After the player has struck the blow and taken the proper steps, he holds his position with his hands on the sled, works his feet rapidly and responds to hand signals by the coach by pursuing right or left. Cones should again be used to designate the five-yard distance on either side of the sled. It is important that the players work up the field, or toward the line of scrimmage, as they pursue right or left.

Sled—Down-the-Line Drill

From a stance the player strikes with his hands, locks out and brings his feet with him. He starts on a pad at one end of the sled. It is desirable to run this drill on a sled that has at least four pads. The player starts on a pad at one end of the sled. From a stance he strikes with the hands, locks out and brings his feet with him. He then backs off the pad slightly, working his feet rapidly and then proceeds down the line, striking each pad as he goes. It is important that he work his feet continuously as he strikes, that he lock out as he strikes each pad and that he keep his shoulder level down throughout the drill. He should finish by pursuing five yards up the field after he strikes the last pad.

PASS-RUSH SLED DRILLS

The best sled to teach pass-rush techniques on is a one-man sled equipped with a pad shaped like the letter T. This type of pad is well designed to execute the power, or bull, rush. It is also the best pad on which to teach any corner of the blocker technique. The T shape simulates the shoulder pad area of the blocker at the top and the lower portion displays the front numbers on a blocker's jersey. These are the critical aiming points for the execution of the various pass-rush techniques. The narrower body on this type of pad allows the rusher to work under the blocker's shoulder pads with the various types of techniques with the inside arm, or the one closest to the blocker.

Power, or Bull, Rush

This technique is executed from the head-up position in a three-point stance. On the snap of the ball, he drives his hands for the outside tips of the numbers, under the shoulder-pad area. He works to lock out his arms, roll his hips into the blow and bring his feet with him. He should have good flexion in the ankles, knees and hips, and his shoulder level should be low and constant throughout the execution of the technique. His initial blow, along with the follow-through of big-muscle involvement, should drive the sled back. The only big step the rusher should take is the first one out of his stance. All other foot movements should consist of short, choppy steps as he drives the sled back.

Grab and Rub

With this drill the rusher reaches for the T pad with his outside arm on the first step out of his stance. He grabs the corner of the pad with his outside arm. At the same time, he takes a big step with his inside leg toward the blocker. He then dips his inside shoulder, exerting pressure against the blocker as he rubs tight to the blocker on his way to the passer.

Grab and Rip

All the elements of the rush are the same except rather than dipping the inside shoulder and rubbing, the rusher rips with his inside arm. As mentioned previously, this rip should resemble an uppercut action with the inside arm.

Grab and Swim

Again, all the elements in the execution of the technique are the same except that the inside arm is used to swim over the corner of the blocker. As described earlier, the swim technique is the same as the overhand type of front crawl stroke used in swimming. Many times, as the hand goes over the corner of the blocker, it will land on the back of the blocker's shoulder pads. The rusher will be able to push on the blocker to help propel him to the passer. There is a very real temptation to raise up as the pass rusher executes the swim technique. That is why it is very important for the coach to emphasize keeping the shoulder level down when a player is executing it.

Counter-Rush

The counter-rush is a finesse type of pass rush in which the rusher starts by faking a pass rush to one side of a blocker and counters that action with a pass-rush move to the opposite side. For example, on his first step the pass rusher steps toward the corner of the pad on the sled to his right. On his second step he reaches with his left hand to grab the tip of the pad to his left. He pulls with his left hand to turn the blocker and at the same time rubs, rips or swims with his right arm and shoulder as he takes his big step past the blocker. This technique should be practiced to both sides so the player develops the ability to counter moves inside and outside by the pass blockers.

It is important to emphasize here that all the pass-rush techniques practiced on the sled should be executed with the pass rushers not raising up. As much as possible, all the momentum of the rusher should be established upfield, or toward the blockers. There should be no lateral moves or steps rushing the passer.

It is advisable to allow the players to substitute a club technique for the grab as they practice rushing on the sled. A club is executed by the rusher driving his hand and arm through the shoulder of the blocker on the side the player is rushing over. The club, like the grab, is used to turn the blocker thereby having the effect of making the corner shorter for the rusher to establish his lane to the passer.

RUN—ONE-ON-ONE DRILLS

These are drills that are executed using two defensive players. One plays the roll of the offensive blocker, the other practices a specific technique the drill is designed to develop. These drills are always run with a tempo that allows the defensive player to feel what the drill is attempting to accomplish. These types of drills should never be run at full speed. The danger is that they might lose all of their relevance as teaching devices if they become toughness or full-speed drills.

One-on-One Hands Drills

With one of the players in a standing position with his hands on his knees, the defensive player gets a fit with his hands on the inside upper tips of the numbers just under the shoulder pads. He next drives the offensive player back a few yards, always keeping his shoulder level lower than that of the blocker. His arms should be locked and he should have big-muscle involvement by maintaining good flexion at the ankles, knees and hips.

One-on-One from a Stance (Two Gap)

The next phase involves both players lining up in a stance. On the offensive player's movement, the defensive man strikes with his hands and calls into play all the elements of the hands technique. It is important that the defensive man finish the drill by knocking the offensive man back. The offensive man should come out of his stance high at less then half speed and allow the defensive man to knock him back.

One-on-One from a Stance (Outside Shade)

Again, with both players in a stance with the defensive player lined up in an outside shade, the offensive man comes off the ball high at less than half speed. The defensive man reacts to the movement by driving his hands to the outside upper tips of the numbers on the front of the blocker's jersey. The defensive man should knock the blocker back as he squeezes, or compresses, the blocker to close the inside gap. In the execution of this technique the aiming point for the defensive man is the same as it is in the two-gap technique. He must constantly be reminded that from this position he is responsible for the outside gap but must also squeeze the inside gap with the offensive lineman's body. The alignments that require this type of technique are a 9, 6, 3 or O strong or weak!

Two-on-One from a Stance

Two offensive players are used for this drill. The defensive lineman lines up in a 6 or 3 alignment. The two offensive players line up adjacent to each other. They double-team block the defensive lineman. The defensive lineman should turn his body to make it narrow. He should work to split the double-team block by driving upfield between the two offensive blockers. The defensive man should be conscious of driving through the blocker who is the drive blocker on the double team. If a defensive end lined up in a 6 technique is being blocked by a tight end and offensive tackle, the defensive end should try to penetrate through the block and pressure against the block by the tight end. Dropping down low toward the ground and staying low gives the defensive player the best chance for success against this type of block.

ONE-ON-ONE PASS RUSH—
HEAD-UP RUSHES

Power, or Bull, Rushes

Just as in the one-on-one run, two-gap technique, the offensive player starts from a stand-up, erect position with his hands on his knees. The defensive man gets a fit with his hands, locks out and drives the offensive man straight back a few yards.

Next, both players line up in a stance with the defensive man aligned head up on the offensive man. The offensive man takes a pass set. The defensive man attacks the blocker as soon as the blocker moves. He, again, drives the blocker back into the passer.

Power Rush and Shed

The next phase involves the pass blocker pass setting. The pass rusher driving his hands into him starts a power, or bull, rush then throws the blocker out of the lane and proceeds to rush the passer.

Counter-Grab or Counter-Club

The offensive and defensive players line up in their stances. The blocker pass sets, and the defensive player starts at the inside corner of the blocker on his first step. His second step is toward the outside corner of the blocker. Simultaneously he grabs or clubs the outside arm or shoulder pad of the blocker with his outside hand and arm. He then rubs, swims or rips with his inside arm as he takes a big step by the blocker.

Push, Pull and Turn

Two defensive players should pair up for this drill. One player serves as a blocker, the other a defender. From the standing position the defensive player gets a fit with his hands on the upper outside tips of the numbers on the front of the blocker's jersey. He starts a power rush and then uses one hand to grab the shoulder pad of the blocker and turn him. He continues to push with the other hand. This drill should finish with the rusher using his rub, rip or swim techniques with the hand and arm opposite the one he grabs with.

Counter-Club

The defensive players are paired up for this drill. The defensive man should be locked up with the blocker, using a rub technique over the outside of the blocker. He then should club the inside shoulder of the blocker with his inside arm. This should be followed with a swim or rip technique as the rusher makes an inside move on the blocker.

Reach Around

This is another of the close-quarter teaching drills in which the rusher is using a rub technique on the blocker. As the defender arrives at a point where he is making his move past the blocker, he should reach for the quarterback with his outside hand. At the same time he should be stepping with his outside leg, striving to point his toes back toward the line of scrimmage. The value of this technique is that, as the quarterback steps up in the pocket, the pass blockers try to ride the rusher past the quarterback. If the rusher attempts to reach for the passer with his inside hand, the blocker will be successful in pushing the rusher past the quarterback. However, if the rusher works to reach the passer with his outside hand and arm and gets his toes pointed back toward the line of scrimmage, the push by the tackle will actually assist the rusher in his attempt to get to the quarterback. (See Photo 9-6.)

PHOTO 9–6
Reach-around technique: Pass rush

ONE-ON-ONE— OUTSIDE PASS RUSHES

These drills are executed with one player serving as an offensive tackle and the other as a defensive end. To execute these drills the offensive tackle lines up in a normal alignment. The defensive end lines up in a wide 6 alignment slightly pointed in. As with the other one-on-one drills, this drill should be started by the movement of the offensive player out of his stance. The defensive man working as a blocker should use his hands to block the defender. These drills should be somewhat competitive. In other words, the man serving as a blocker should try to pass block the rusher. The rusher should finish every drill by using the reach-around technique that involves his attempting to grab the passer with his outside arm as he gets his toes pointed back toward the line of scrimmage.

Speed Rush Upfield and Rub, Rip or Swim

The outside pass rusher establishes an aiming point behind the center at the depth he expects to meet the passer on his drop. The angle of his alignment should aim him, in a straight line, to that point. On movement by the tackle he should attempt to sprint past the offensive tackle. He will use the rub technique by leaning into the blocker with his inside arm or shoulder to shorten or collapse his route to the passer. He will also use the rip and swim techniques with the inside arm to prevent the blocker from grabbing it.

Upfield Counter

The counters to the upfield speed rushes are the counter-grab or counter-club moves. With these pass-rush techniques the defensive end threatens the offensive tackle upfield with speed. He forces the blocker to compromise his squared-up relationship with the line of scrimmage by turning or crossing his feet; he then makes an inside pass-rush move. It is important that the rusher be patient and not make the inside move until he is parallel with the upfield shoulder of the blocker. This ensures that the blocker will not be able to recover and prevent the rusher from beating him inside.

As the rusher reaches the upfield shoulder of the blocker, he reaches with his inside hand and arm to grab or club the inside shoulder of the blocker. By grabbing or clubbing the blocker, the rusher will turn him, thereby opening the inside rush lane. The rusher should then rip or swim with his outside arm as he goes past the blocker.

TWO-ON-TWO— TWO-MAN GAMES

The initial stages of practice on two-man games should be done with four defensive players. Two serve as offensive blockers and the remaining two as pass rushers. The quick games, as well as the delay games, should be taught in this type of environment. The offensive players should use quick, or short, pass sets as well as deep sets. This allows the rushers working on the games to practice them against the various types of pass protections they will face. The two-on-two games will involve the 4-3 defensive end and tackle.

To work on tackle–tackle games in the 4-3 defense another offensive blocker should be added. This additional blocker will play the role of the center. Having a center lined up between the guards provides the exact spacings they will face when executing these games against an offensive team.

To work on end/nose tackle–tackle games in a 3-4 defense an additional player is required. Again, to get the actual spacing involved, the offensive players should consist of a tackle, guard and center. The extra player is the guard since in this defense the end normally lines up over the tackle and the nose tackle over the center.

THREE-MAN GAMES

In order to teach and practice three-man games, the offensive players need to include a tackle, two guards and a center. This group of players will provide the proper personnel spacing to run any combination of three-man games.

The drills outlined in this chapter provide vehicles for the teaching of every technique essential to playing effectively on the defensive line of scrimmage. I have used most of these drills over the past forty-two years, continually modifying and upgrading them. I really believe in the phase method of teaching technique. I feel the skilled coach will continuously look for ways to break down the techniques he wants to teach into phases or steps that cause the player to learn at a high level.

10

Defensive Line Checklist and Opponent Evaluation Form

DEFENSIVE LINE CHECKLIST

One of the most critical aspects of coaching is the ability to organize practice time to cover all the areas that need to be addressed. Obviously, it is impossible to cover every technique and run every drill every day. However, it is imperative that the position coach develop a priority list. This list should consist of all the things that are essential to do every day. Another way to put this is, the list should consist of the most important techniques and skills essential to playing on the defensive line.

In my opinion, a defensive line coach should work on the four most important aspects of defensive line play every day. These are movement, takeoff, hands and pass rush. I would worry about the competence of a defensive line coach if he did not have these four areas at the top of his priority list.

DEFENSIVE LINE TECHNIQUE & DRILL CHECK LIST

Practice Number

	1	2	3	4	5	6	7	8	9	10	11	12	13
Stance													
Movement													
Warm-up Drills													
High Knee Jog													
Carioca													
Crossovers on the Line													
Quick Feet Hip Turn													
Back Pedal, Turn													
Wave Drill													
Take off Drill													
Take off & Wave Combined													
Bag Drills													
High Step Over Forward													
Side Shuffle Over Bags													
Quick Feet Over Dummies													
Forward-Backward between Dummies													
Individual Waves Over Dummies													
Sled Drills													
Hands From Knees													
Hands Up Position													
Down Line Hands													
Pass Rush Sled													
Power													
Grab or Club & Rub													
Grab or Club & Rip													
Grab or Club & Swim													
Counter Rush													
Run One-on-one Drills													
Base Block - 2 Gap													
Base Block - Outside Technique													
Reach Block Right or Left													

DEFENSIVE LINE TECHNIQUE & DRILL CHECK LIST

Practice Number

	1	2	3	4	5	6	7	8	9	10	11	12	13
Run Two on One Blocks													
Double Team													
Reach and Scoop Block													
Run Three on Two (Tackles vs. Guards & Center)													
Trap													
Base Blocks													
Draw Block													
Pass One-on-one													
Power													
Corner or Edge of Blocker													
Counter Rush													
Pass Two-on-two Pass Rush Game													
Tackle-Tackle Quick Games													
End-Tackle Quick Games													
End-Tackle Delay Games													
Tackle-End Games													
Halfline Blk'ing Scheme Recognition													
Base Block													
Reach and Scoop													
Trap													
Lead													

The best way to ensure that all necessary areas are covered is to develop a checklist. I have included this list as part of this chapter. It is especially important that this type of list be developed to be used during, what I like to call, critical teaching periods like spring ball and early fall camp as well as two-a-day practice sessions.

DEFENSIVE LINE OPPONENT EVALUATION FORM

Over the years, I have devised a form that is designed to assist defensive linemen in the film study of their opponents. It has been my experience that players do not innately know how to study their opponents on tape, so this form is meant to be a guide in this regard. If a defensive lineman can fill in a good number of blanks on this form after he has studied his opponent, he should be well prepared to compete against him. I also encourage players to add to this form as they look at game tapes after they have played an opponent. The coach should keep a copy of these forms since they will serve as a permanent record of an opponent. This will help the individual player and coach prepare for an opponent in future games.

The top part of the form should be filled out before the evaluation process begins. If a player's position involves him playing over more than one player, he should use a study sheet for each player. The name of the player's team, the name of the player, his number and position should all be filled out along with the height and weight.

The following is a brief explanation of each section of the form along with suggested observations and preparation questions.

1. Stance

The type of stance the opponent uses and how it changes in various situations is important. Specific factors like how much weight he has forward and width of the feet are all important!

2. Splits

The type of splits between the player we are evaluating and his teammates is what we are seeking here. How do these splits vary on the various types of plays or situations? For example: Many times players will line up with very tight splits when they are running wide plays and use bigger splits when they are running inside. On the other hand, very often teams will use wider splits to the side of the formation where the play is designed to go and tighter splits away from the play side in order to make better use of cutoff, backside scoop or slip blocks.

3. Run Technique

This section is used to evaluate those factors involved with the style of run blocking an opponent uses. How the blocker comes off the ball, high or low, or how he uses his hands in blocking are all important factors here. Whether a player sets back in his stance or lines up deeper when he pulls are all important things to look for.

4. Play-Action Technique

The type of blocking action used—do they aggressively block play action and make it look like a running play? Do they hinge the backside or set back?

5. Drop-Back Passes

Do they vary their splits when they are going to drop-back pass? Is the opponent a soft or firm pass setter? Does he use his hands? Does he turn or stay square with the line of scrimmage? Does he punch and recoil? Will he firm up on a bull rush? How does he handle countermoves? How deep does the quarterback set to throw the ball? How fast does he get away from the center? Does he cheat with a little step just before the snap? Do they man or zone block games and stunts?

6. Short Yardage

What type of blocking technique does the opponent use in short yardage? Are there tighter splits? Does he come off the ball lower in short yardage? Some players do.

7. Goal Line

We are looking for the same factors here that we are looking for in short yardage.

8. Running Game (formation and plays)

In this section we want the player to identify the specific types of runs the opponent runs from their various formations. We would also like to have the player identify the toughest running play for him to read. Plays where the opponent uses influence blocks or where there is counter-action or misdirection are usually these types of plays. The runs they use in long-yardage situations is also information the player should know. Whether a team runs draws or traps in long yardage is absolutely essential information for the defensive linemen to know.

9. Draw Downs

Some teams run draw plays only in a very narrow window of down-and-distance situations. Formations many times determine the probability of a draw play being run. This is all very important information.

10. Screens

When teams run screens, whether in specific down-and-distance situations or from specific formations, is also a very important part of game preparation knowledge.

11. Pass Protections They Use

A player should be trained to look for the specific types of pass protection his opponents will use. Will they slide the protection strong or weak or will they respond by bringing the uncovered lineman out?

12. Pass-Rush Games

What games have the best chance for success after watching tapes all week? Why does it look as though they will be successful?

DEFENSIVE LINE OPPONENT EVALUATION FORM

TEAM _____
NAME _____   HT._____ WT._____
NO. _____
POSITION _____

1. STANCE _____
2. SPLITS Run_____
           Play Action_____
           Drop Back_____
           Goal Line_____
           Short Yardage_____
           Plays To_____
           Plays Away_____
3. RUN TECHNIQUE: Evaluation Coming Off
           Hand Use_____
           Position_____
           Combination Blocks_____
           (Slips-Powers, Etc.)_____
           Pull_____
           Trap_____
           Down Block_____
           Reach Block_____
           Influence Blocks_____
           Backside Scoop or Man_____
4. PLAY ACTION TECHNIQUE:
           Play Side_____
           Back Side_____
5. DROP BACK:
           Splits_____
           QB Set_____
           Hands_____
           Feet_____
           Games (How they pick up)_____
           Technique_____
           Scheme_____

6. SHORT YARDAGE (Tech.) _____

7. GOAL LINE (Tech.) _____

8. RUNNING GAME: (Formation & Play ie: I - 18 Toss, Sp. 22 Trap)
   8 & 9 Hole Plays: Weak _ie: Op. Slant 18_____
                     Strong _ie: I - 18 Toss_____
   6 & 7 Hole Plays: Weak _____
                     Strong _ie: Sp. 26 Power_____
   4 & 5 Hole Plays: Weak _____
                     Strong _ie: Sp. 24 Dive_____
   2 & 3 Hole Plays: Weak _____
                     Strong _ie: Sp. 22 Trap_____
   0 & 1 Hole Plays: Weak _____
                     Strong _____
   Toughest Plays for You to Read: _____
   _____
   _____

   Runs They Like to Use Vs. Nickel & Other Long Yardage: _____
   _____
   _____

9. WHAT DOWNS DO THEY DRAW ON? _____

10. WHAT DOWNS DO THEY SCREEN ON? _____

11. WHAT PASS PROTECTIONS DO THEY USE:
    Regular Situations _____
    Nickel Situations _____

12. WHAT PASS RUSH & GAMES LOOK BEST TO YOU:
    From 4-3 _____
    Over or Under _____
    3 Man Games _____

COACHING TEAM DEFENSE
Second Edition
Fritz Shurmur

Fritz Shurmur, the defensive coordinator for the Green Bay Packers, has expanded the original edition of his book, which is considered by many to be one of the best books ever written on football defense. This excellent guide provides a solid fundamental approach to understanding and executing the basic concepts of team defense.

> "**Coaching Team Defense, Second Edition,** *was and is a must for all coaches, players, and even fans who want to understand real football.*"
>
> Matt Millen
> TV Football Analyst
> Fox Sports

> "*Fritz Shurmur's* **Coaching Team Defense—Second Edition** *expands on the first edition with diagrams, tackling and tackling drills, zone pass coverages, and everything not covered in the initial book. An excellent book for coaches at any level with explanations of all defensive areas.*"
>
> George Perles
> Former Head Coach
> Michigan State U.

> "*Fritz Shurmur's new edition of* **Coaching Team Defense** *is an expanded version of truly one of the best books I've read regarding defensive football. The new book is full of clean and concise details of coaching defense that coaches of all levels will benefit from. This is Fritz's best work yet!*"
>
> Tom Hayes
> Assistant Coach
> Washington Redskins

Fritz Shurmur is a coaching veteran of more than 40 seasons, including 22 in the NFL. Coach Shurmur is also the author of *The Eagle Five-Linebacker Defense.*

$12.00

COACHING THE DEFENSIVE BACKFIELD
Greg McMackin

Coaching the Defensive Backfield is a thorough study of all the fundamentals, techniques and drills you will need to produce a successful secondary. You are shown the specific techniques and drills you will need to produce game-winning execution.

Coaching the Defensive Backfield allows you to prepare your secondary defenders through a complete plan concerning skills, techniques and game-like drills that will help you to produce a fundamentally sound, aggressive and exciting defensive backfield.

> *"Greg McMackin is one of the best in the business. His book is very informative and every coach should have one."*
>
> Dennis Erickson
> Head Coach—Seattle Seahawks

> *"This is the most comprehensive book I've read on secondary play...* Coaching the Defensive Backfield *will educate the coach and stimulate the player."*
>
> Ron McBride
> Head Coach—U. of Utah

> *"Pursuit, tackling, two deep, three deep, zone, man, blitz, bump...this book has it all.* **Coaching the Defensive Backfield** *is a must for coaches at all levels."*
>
> Steve Axman
> Head Coach
> Northern Arizona U.

Greg McMackin is the defensive coordinator for the Seattle Seahawks. Immediately prior to this, he served in the same capacity at the University of Miami where his defenses led the nation in several categories. Coach McMackin has coached successfully for more than 20 years at the high school, college and professional levels.

$12.00

THE EAGLE FIVE-LINEBACKER DEFENSE
Fritz Shurmur

Fritz Shurmur, defensive coordinator of the Green Bay Packers, presents a unique and innovative defensive scheme which is based on solid principles, techniques and drills that are applicable to any defensive plan at any level of play. This unique defensive concept allows coaches to attack today's wide-open offenses rather than having to react.

> *"If you want an exceptional version of modern-day defensive play,* **The Eagle Five-Linebacker Defense** *by Fritz Shurmur is must reading."*
>
> Bill Parcells
> Head Football Coach
> New England Patriots
> Winner of Two Super Bowls

> *"***The Eagle Five-Linebacker Defense** *is a clear, concise, step-by-step discussion of an important trend in defensive football. If you want to be in the mainstream of defensive thinking, this book is must reading."*
>
> Lloyd Carr
> Head Football Coach
> U. of Michigan

> *"Fritz Shurmur's* **The Eagle Five-Linebacker Defense** *is a tremendous addition to any coach's library at any level of play. It is an excellent book on a unique way of utilizing defensive personnel in modern-day football."*
>
> Tom Hayes
> Assistant Coach
> Washington Redskins

Fritz Shurmur is a coaching veteran of 40 years, including the last 20 in the NFL. Recognized as a defensive innovator, Coach Shurmur served as defensive coordinator with the Phoenix Cardinals and the Los Angeles Rams before coming to Green Bay. He is also the author of *Coaching Team Defense, Second Edition*.

$12.00

DEFENSING THE DELAWARE WING-T, Bob Kenig ($12.00)

This coaching guide offers a successful and easily teachable answer to the dynamic Wing-T. The innovative use of the 3-4 "Slant" and "Read Blitz" presents major problems for this offense. All aspects of installing the "Slant" and "Read Blitz" are detailed, and the actual application of these techniques is explained and diagramed against the basic Wing-T plays. Bob Kenig has coached successfully at both the high school and college levels. He is presently coaching at Widener University where he has helped them reach the NCAA Division III playoffs each of the past two seasons.

FOOTBALL'S EXPLOSIVE MULTI-BONE ATTACK, Tony DeMeo ($12.00)

Coach DeMeo, who is presently the head coach at Washburn University, is widely recognized as one of the most innovative offensive coaches in football today. His Multi-Bone combines the explosiveness of the Veer, the power of the I, the deception and misdirection of the Wing-T, the ball control of the Wishbone and the wide-open play of the Pro Drop-back Passing game. This book shows you how to tie together the best of these offenses into one easy-to-learn package.

COACHING RUN-AND-SHOOT FOOTBALL, Al Black ($12.00)

This unique guide presents an exciting attack that can enhance your present offense or stand alone. Coach Black, a successful 30-year coaching veteran whose career includes a very impressive 149-41-2 high school record, gives you all the run-and-shoot pass routes, plus blocking schemes, a complementary offense, a one-back running game, and much more.

DEFENSING THE RUN AND SHOOT, Bob Kenig ($12.00)

Bob Kenig, author of the very popular **DEFENSING THE DELAWARE WING-T**, gives you the tools to derail the explosive Run and Shoot. The defensive system in this book employs both odd and even fronts, which are skillfully utilized with man-to-man, zone and combination defenses. The book also provides you with an extensive blitz package, plus an invaluable chapter that shows you how to disguise the defenses. Coach Kenig recently completed his latest book, *Football's Modern 4-3 Defense*, available from Harding Press January, 1997 ($18.00).

HARDING PRESS, INC.
P.O. BOX 141
HAWORTH, N.J. 07641
(201) 767-7114
FAX: (201) 767-8745

ORDER FORM

# of COPIES	TITLE	TOTAL PRICE

Postage & Handling: SUBTOTAL _____

Order	U.S.	Outside U.S.
Under $25.00	$3.00	$ 7.75
$ 25.00 − $ 49.99	$4.75	$10.50
$ 50.00 − $ 74.99	$6.25	$11.75
$ 75.00 − $ 99.99	$7.50	$12.75
$100.00 − $149.99	$8.25	$13.50
$150.00 − $199.99	$9.00	$14.50
$200.00 +	$9.75	$15.00

NJ Residents −
Add 6% Sales Tax _____

P & H _____

TOTAL _____

EACH ORDER MUST BE ACCOMPANIED BY CHECK, M.O., P.O., or CREDIT CARD info

COACH'S NAME _____

ADDRESS _____

_____

CITY _____ **STATE** _____ **ZIP** _____

PHONE # (____) _____
             area code

MASTERCARD/VISA: _____
                      Card #   Exp. Date

_____
Signature